THE PROOF TRAP

JACK CAZELL

'That which is true, but cannot be proven so, becomes not true.

And that which is not true, yet is proven to be true, becomes the truth

Table of Contents

The Proof Trap

Part 1. Injustice

David Croswell and his daughter Judy sat silently in the second row of the Gloucester County Court. The Jury was out. The man charged with his wife's murder sat silently in the witness box. His name was Daniel Price, a labourer on construction sites around Gloucester. He looked decidedly awkward in a suit, and the tattoos on his neck showed above his collar. Even in a suit and tie, he still looked decidedly like a ruffian that was best avoided. *Flash as a rat with a gold tooth.* David thought. *It just goes to show - you can't polish a turd.*

David observed what he thought was a wry smile on his face. He knew it was a long shot that he would be convicted. The evidence was not strong enough. Circumstantial. DNA tests were inconclusive. The whole prosecution was based on possibilities and likely scenarios. They had enough to strongly implicate Price and have him charged, but on the back of a 'Not Guilty' plea, the Jury would be hard-pressed to convict. It seemed plainly obvious to the man that led the investigation–Senior Detective Inspector Michael Judd, that Price was the killer, but 'proof beyond reasonable doubt' seemed elusive. His alibi was that he was with his girlfriend at the time of the murder. She had corroborated it. Of course, she would.

****

The whole ordeal of the past nine months had not gone well for David. One Friday evening, Marion, his wife of 34 years, had gone for a twilight walk around the quiet village of Maisemore. They had settled here three years previous, once their daughter Judy had finished her law degree at Gloucestershire University, and married her long-time sweetheart. The move was partly for a quieter place to work from at home and partly to downsize their house and give themselves a financial buffer so David could pursue his writing interest after his retirement from 36 years of teaching English Literature at King's.

His life had been fairly uneventful, born and raised in Gloucestershire, studied at King's where he first met Marion when the school admitted girls in 1969. David was tall and athletic, an accomplished cricketer during his school days. Lean and lanky Marion played netball for King's in high school, and despite her modest (by netball standards) 5'7" height, she was good enough to go to a higher level, but other interests got in the way. They had both finished their schooling at King's then had gone their separate ways for their tertiary education. After David had completed his teaching degree, he landed a job back at King's. He shortly thereafter discovered that Marion had also returned from London to take up a management position with a local retail firm. Their reconnection in familiar territory ignited a romance that had been quietly simmering during their school days. They married, and settled into a low-key, conservative life, raising an only child, Judy.

To any outside observer, David was a model citizen – a teacher at a prestigious school, with a professional wife and perfect daughter, a volunteer for countless community events, and King's senior cricket team coach.

What no one ever saw, and David never much spoke about, was his interest in – or even fascination with – crime and the criminal mind. He had long wanted to be a writer of crime fiction, but never had the time. So, as soon as he could financially afford it, he retired from teaching, sold their Denmark Road home in Gloucester, and moved to Maisemore, a few miles away.

The properties in Maisemore and nearby Highnam were considerably cheaper than in suburban Gloucester. The downside was that they housed pockets with a lower socio-economic class of residents.

****

Normally, he would have gone with Marion on a walk, but on this occasion, his knee was giving him some grief, so he stayed home. Two hours later, she hadn't returned. He feared something was wrong. He called her phone several times. No answer. He called the police. Apparently, you can't list a person as 'missing' until they've been gone for 24 hours. So, he went and searched for her himself.

A half-hour later, he found her. Well, he found her body, halfway down the bank of the 'lake' in the bushes alongside her usual walking path that ran between Church Road and The Rudge. He called the police again. This time they did take notice. He sat alongside her body and cried until the police arrived. It was four in the morning before he got home.

"WHY??" he shouted as he stormed around the house. "WHO COULD DO THIS?" It was surreal. He sat staring at the floor. Body and mind numb. He could see his body but could not feel that it was there. He thought he heard Marion at the door. But he had seen her dead body just hours earlier. His beloved Marion was not coming home. Her body was cold in the mortuary. He wanted to hug and kiss her and tell her everything would be ok. But it never would be ok. What has happened? How could it happen? Who did this? Surely, the police would find the culprit. But Marion would never walk through the door again and ask him if he wanted a cup of tea. He would never feel her warm embrace or her arms around him as they slept.

The lights of the living room were on, but it felt like darkness was closing in on him from all sides. Should he call Judy now? Wake her and tell her that her mother has been murdered? David felt like he was about to vomit and rushed to the bathroom. Leaning over the basin with both hands on the rim. He felt cold, although sweat dripped from his face into the bowl, slowly trickling to the plughole. He looked in the mirror and could hardly recognise the face looking back at him. He didn't vomit.

The tap was running. David didn't remember turning it on. He scooped some cold water in his cupped hands and brought it to his face. The cold water jolted him back to reason.

He would call Judy in the morning. Judy lived a few miles away in Gloucester. She was 7 months pregnant and needed the rest. Best not to wake her now.

David lay awake, feeling a yawning emptiness in the bed beside him. Eventually, exhaustion conquered adrenalin, and he slept. Sunlight streamed through the window when he woke, suddenly remembering the night. He snapped a look at Marion's side of the bed in the vain hope that it was all a bad dream. He lay staring at the ceiling.

"FUCK!"

"Fuck, fuck, fuck, fuck, fuck, FAAARRRKKK!!" David shouted to the empty room.

He had to call Judy now. It would be on the morning news for sure. It was not a call he was looking forward to.

"Hello, Dad"

"Hello, Jude."

"What's the matter, dad?" Judy instantly sensed the sadness in his voice.'

"It's Mum." David burst into tears. "She's...... she's been murdered."

There was a few moments' silence as Judy processed what she had just heard.

"What?! How?! I'm coming over."

****

The post-mortem revealed that Marion had died from a brain haemorrhage caused by a single blow to the head with a blunt object–most likely a tree branch. She had died where she fell. The police found her phone and purse a few meters away in the bushes. Any cash she had was gone, but credit cards remained. Police concluded that the motive was robbery. David could not reconcile the senselessness of taking a life for what was probably less than 50 pounds.

The news rocked the village, and there were abundant rumours and theories of what had happened. Over the coming weeks, David's sadness turned to anger, and anger turned to an obsession for vengeance. But who did this? He was poised to fire with nothing to aim at.

The police investigation identified a number of suspects, but in the end, it came down to just two men who were known to have been in the area before Marion's murder, Daniel Price and William Ogden. They had been drinking at the White Horse Inn and left quite intoxicated around 9.40. They maintained that they went straight home. And both their partners had confirmed that they got to their respective homes at around 9.45. Marion's estimated time of death was 10 – 10.15. Both men were known for violent turns when drunk, and Price had served 18 months in jail for GBH and robbery three years earlier. He had a long history of violent offences usually associated with being drunk. Ogden had served 6 months for aggravated assault, after a pub brawl over a football game, left his opponent with a broken jaw and fractured cheekbone.

Their direct route home from the Inn would not have taken them along the track where Marion was found, but they could certainly have taken that route if they felt inclined, and video from the inn carpark showed them heading in that direction when they left.

The investigation was at a dead end until Price was overheard in a drunken state, saying how he had clubbed the woman and stolen her money. "Easy 75 pounds!" Price had quipped. Of course, once he had sobered up, he denied all knowledge of even saying such things, blaming the drink for creating a fantasy on the back of the murder.

In the absence of anything else to go on, both men were arrested and charged.

Three months later, the police dropped the charges against Ogden, due to lack of any substantial evidence. Inspector Michael Judd conducted the concluding interview and escorted Ogden from the building. David was disappointed but not surprised. He had been told by Judd that Ogden would be released so he came to the station to see it. The smug look on Ogden's face as he left the station told David he was guilty of something.

The prosecution took more time to build a case against Price and had some more circumstantial evidence. Mud on his boots matched that of the murder scene – but that didn't prove he was there at the time of the attack. A footprint near the body matched the size and made of the boots he was wearing that night, but more than half the workers in the town would have size 11, Doc Martens. All pointed to the fact that he could have done it but didn't prove that he did. Now his case was being heard.

The prosecuting lawyer had made good use of the fact that the evidence pointed to the high likelihood that the footprint was Price's, and the mud on his boots matched that at the murder scene. And he was known to be in the area at the time. But honestly, he had no conclusive proof. Price had not left any DNA on the body or the purse. The publican had noted that Price put gloves on before he left the Inn that night. It was quite cold that night–for May.

The defence argued that there would be no reason for Price to walk the long way around to his home, even though the video from the Inn carpark security camera showed him heading in that direction when he left.

Still, David held some hope that the Jury would see through the lies and convict him. Judy sat to his left and held tightly to his arm.

The Jury returned to the courtroom and took their seats. The foreman stood at the front.

"Have you reached a verdict beyond all reasonable doubt?" the Judge asked.

"We have, your Honour."

"What be your verdict?"

"We find the defendant Not Guilty."

A cheer erupted from the back of the courtroom, and Daniel Price was led from the witness box to join his family and supporters. David sat silently starring at the floor. There was no justice for Marion. No Justice for him and Judy.

"Come on, dad," Judy said to him, standing up. "Let's go. James is meeting me outside with baby David. I'm near bursting."

They turned into the aisle as the cheering mob was exiting the courtroom, with Price at the back of the pack. He turned to David and smiled a smug smile. Then addressing his mob, he said, "To the Dick, everyone. The drinks are on me. It's not every day you get away with murder." He turned a wink towards David and Judy.

David stopped in his tracks, and hatred boiled up inside him. *Daniel Price will not get away with murder.*

Outside the courthouse, Chief Inspector Michael Judd was waiting for David.

"I'm sorry, Dave. I wish I could have got something more solid to go on."

David looked sorrowfully at the inspector. "You did your best. What do you think, Mick? Do you think he did it?"

"Not much doubt in my mind. Unfortunately, the court needs *proof—beyond reasonable doubt.* That's what we weren't able to get on him. I'm just hoping that he will slip up, make a confession to someone. Maybe guilt will get the better of him one day."

"I'm not going to hold my breath for that day, Mick. You saw how smug he was. I'd fucking kill the prick if he started sprouting about it."

"Careful, Dave. Remember who you're talking to. But I feel your frustration. Want to go for a drink?"

"Not today, Mick. Judy's waiting for me in the car. She's feeding the baby. We'll have a quiet afternoon together."

"If you hear anything, let me know. You know what I mean."

"For sure. See you around."

Michael Judd sensed the anger in David's eyes and watched him as he headed for the carpark. *Was that just an angry comment? Would David be capable of killing Price?* He didn't think so, but he'd been in the job long enough to know that you just can't tell with some people. Although he had known David from occasional professional contacts over the past three decades, the investigation had bought them closer, to the point that Judd considered him more than an acquaintance, bordering on a friend. But coppers rarely have close friends outside the job; there is always some distance.

David waited while Judy fed the baby in the car. Her husband, James, got out of the driver's side.

"Fucking unfair," he said.

"Sorry James, I can't talk about it. I haven't got words to describe Price."

"I can think of one," James said as he watched the last of Price's supporters leave the carpark. "Cunt."

David chuckled at the uncharacteristic profanity from James.

"Let's go with fucking lying, low-life, murdering, useless, scumbag cunt." David said, checking that Judy did not hear him. "Justice will be done eventually, James," David said, returning to seriousness. "I'll make damn sure of it."

"How so?"

"I don't know for sure. But I know it will."

Judy got out of the car and put the sleeping baby in the capsule on the rear seat.

"I'll see you later, Dave," James said as he opened the car door.

"Bye, love. I'll be home around 7, yeah." Judy kissed James on the lips.

"I'll drive," Judy said, taking the car keys from David.

David and Judy got into David's S Series Jag and headed out from the carpark.

Mick Judd squinted into the sunlight as he watched David and Judy drive out of the carpark, extenuating the wrinkles around his eyes and mouth, making him look older than his 56 years. The 'job' takes its toll. Late nights working, dead-end cases, bitter disappointments—like today's. He felt for David and Judy. No justice for Marion's murder. No closure. But he had been there too many times before. The life of a detective is swimming in a sea of disappointment with occasional success to keep you going - just enough to turn up the next day.

Mick recalled the night he got the call. When the phone rings after 10.00 at night, he knows someone has died. This one was harder than usual. He knew Marion .... and David – everyone in Gloucester did. Local identities in their own understated way. Always there at any event, quietly working in the background, volunteering was a habit. David had worked at Kings for so long most of the town had had him for a teacher or played cricket with or against him. Marion was just one of those people everyone liked, who always had time for anyone. This was a case he really wanted to solve. Such a beautiful person so senselessly struck down. The culprit had to be found and punished.

He was sure Price did it. There was no-one else who could have. It was simply not plausible that, in the quiet village of Maisemore, anyone else could have been on that path and killed Marion. Unfortunately, the absence of any other suspect doesn't prove he did it. Even an extremely high likelihood that he did it isn't good enough for a conviction. Mick felt he had let David down. Price was guilty – he knew it. He had to pay for it ..... somehow.. Sadness mingled with anger swirled in his head. Another failure. Another open wound. *This fucken job will kill me.* He turned to cross the street, looking up at the window of his office on the third floor of the building in front of him. *That office is a prison of a whole different kind. This job is a prison .... A Trap. I'm caught in a fucken 'proof trap'. Trapped in this fucken stupid world of trying to find 'proof' for shit that I already know is true. And when I can't find it, I stay fucken trapped ...... forever. Whose stupid idea was it to go into the job anyway? My old man. He thought it would be good for his status in the community – having a copper for a son. Should never have listened to the dopey old prick. If he'd had any fucken idea how frustrating it can be, he'd never have suggested it. Scumbags like fucken Price. They make your skin creep just to look at them. Then they walk ... happy as larks. I'm going to bring that prick down ... one day I'll get the bastard.*

Duty was calling...... other cases...... he had to let this one go, leave it hanging like something dead on a rope. His phone rang. It was Dave.

"Mick, I just want to let you know that I don't blame you, ok? You did what you could. You're a good detective, Mick. Don't let this do you over. Karma will sort it out in the end; it always does."

"Thanks, Dave. I wish I shared your belief in Karma. Sometimes, I think these pricks just get away with it. I'll be alright, see you around. Maybe we could have that drink later."

"Yeah, let's make that happen. Bye, Mick."

Mick crossed the street and disappeared into the police station.

Part 2. Redemption

Three months later...

David made his way up the sand-covered steps from the beach towards the cottage near Port Talbot he had rented for a few days. The cottage was an old farm workers' cottage. The Jones's had bought the main farmhouse and cottage some years ago when the farmland was swallowed up by an empire-building neighbour. They restored both buildings and let the cottage for holidaymakers and recluse seekers, and lived in the modest farmhouse a hundred yards or so further along the track from the cottage. The road was sealed up to the old farm gate, but the last 100 yards or so to the cottage was dirt – more sand, really. Windswept trees lined the sides of the track to the cottage, where they abruptly stopped, leaving the farmhouse much more exposed to the Atlantic winds.

Unfortunately, Mr. Jones (Tom) had died shortly after the renovation was complete. David often thought it was the stress of the renovation work that killed him. The one-bedroom cottage was stone of the traditional two-room gable roof style, with a lean-to section on the back and a narrow verandah on the front. The original thatched roof had been replaced with an iron roof. The windows were small, and many decades had passed since the last time they could be opened. There was a stone fireplace at one end of the building, a small kitchen, bathroom, and laundry in the lean-to. A small storeroom had been attached to the back of the bathroom. It was well appointed but wore the tell-tale signs that it was renovated on a shoestring budget.

The sun had risen, and the cottage cast a long shadow over the path. He turned to gaze out over the ocean, the rising wind blowing his straggled hair. Towering storm clouds loomed over the sea, some miles offshore.

"You had better get that fire going!" came the familiar voice of Mrs. Jones from the path behind him. "It's going to blow up quite a storm."

Mrs. J. continued down the path towards the beach.

"I will," David called after her, and he turned to the cottage. His boots were covered in sand, so he took them off at the door and left them outside.

Inside, he lit the pre-set fire in the hearth and watched the flames rise. He was tired – and hungry. *I'd better have something to eat before I sleep*, he thought and poured muesli into a bowl. Just then, his phone rang. The caller's name read 'Michael Judd–Gloucester CID.'

"Mick! To what do I owe the pleasure?"

"I'm wondering if you can let me in—I've been knocking on your door for ten minutes."

"I'd love to, Mick, but unfortunately, I'm not there. I'm down here near Port Talbot for a few days. What's this all about?"

"I see. You're at Port Talbot." Mick pondered. This was already throwing him off track.

"What's this about, Mick?" David persisted.

"It's about Daniel Price."

"That Arse-hole! Who's he killed now?"

"No one. He's dead."

"Dead!? That's the best news I've heard for a year. I hope his death was slow and painful."

"Actually, it seems it was very quick. He was murdered last night."

"Murdered? Are you sure? Not accidental death? Death by misadventure?"

"We're pretty sure it was murder. Hands and feet bound with zip ties and a knife wound to the chest. What do you think, Mr. Crime Writer, sound like Murder to you?"

"It has some of the classic hallmarks by the sound of it. This is great. Murdered! Fantastic! It couldn't happen to a nicer Cunt. You've made my day, Mick. Any suspects?"

"Well, that's why I'm here. Our only suspect is *you* at this point."

"Me?! Why would you think I did it?"

"It's obvious, isn't it? You think he killed Marion. You would want revenge."

"I'm bloody sure he killed Marion. And I don't think you have any doubts either. But I'm over here at Port Talbot."

"Quite, that does put a bit of a dent in my theory. There's something else, though – actually two things. You know what date it is today?"

"Are you serious, Mick? 14th May. The day Marion was taken from me by some low-life scumbag. How will I ever forget it? What is the other thing?"

"The place where Price was murdered. The same place Marion was…... attacked. It just seems too much of a coincidence, don't you think?"

David considered his next words.

"Sounds more like poetic justice to me. That is an uncanny coincidence, though. What do you make of it, Mick?"

"At this point, I don't know what to think. I was hoping you might be able to help me make some sense of it. Can I come and see you?"

"For sure, this place is not easy to find, though. When you get to Swansea, call me, and I'll talk you in."

"I'll be there in about 3 hours. I need to brief my team before I leave. Have the kettle on."

"I was more thinking Champagne, given this news. See you then."

David sat in a floral armchair and thought through the scenario. Mick would be here in 3 hours—Plenty of time. Even still, his heart rate increased a little.

He finished his breakfast and did a bit of tidying up. Washed the dishes, wiped down the benches. Some things had to be set right before Mick arrived. With everything done, he kicked off his slippers and lay on the bed fully clothed with the covers pulled back. It was warm in the cottage now. He had time for about 2 hours of sleep. He set his phone alarm for 2 hours' time and dozed off. He was beat - exhausted.

A little less than 2 hours later, he was jolted from his slumber by the sound of his phone ringing. It was Mick. He was here already.

"Hey Dave, I'm here. I'm outside the Town Hall. Which way do I go?"

David was struggling to regain consciousness and tried to sound awake.

"Head east out of town on the A483 then turn onto the M4—I'm actually just out of Port Talbot. Call back when you get south of Port Talbot railway station. I'll talk you in as you drive."

David tidied his bed, washed his face, re-stoked the fire, filled the kettle, and pushed the 'on' lever down.

David was waiting at the window when Michael Judd arrived outside the cottage. The storm had blown up, and rain squalls came and went every few minutes. The sea was now barely visible in the mist and rain, and what could be seen was all white-caps and foam. The wind howled around and rattled the old cottage. He opened the door for the detective as he rushed from the car with his coat collar pulled up over his neck.

"Thanks, David," he said, taking off his coat and hanging it in the entrance. "Nice and warm in here."

"Got the fire going especially for you." David quipped with a grin.

"Have a seat, Mick," David said, gesturing to the sofa. "Tea? Coffee? How do you have it?"

"Coffee, black, strong."

"Of course." David watched Mick as he made the coffee and an Earl Grey tea for himself. Mick was carefully perusing the room and David while pretending to be disinterested.

"Jeez, Dave, you've lost a bit of weight since I saw you last!"

"Yeah. Been on a health kick. Judy's been on my back about my weight for ages. You know the guilt game – '*You're getting on for 60 now, dad. You've got to take your health seriously. I want you around for a long time.'* She's turning me into a Vegan exercise nut."

"Well, it certainly looks to be doing you good. What have you been doing for exercise?"

"You won't believe this – Karate. I'm working on a brown belt. So far. You should try it, Mick. Good for body and mind. It would get you off those blood pressure pills. The Karate school is only two streets away from your office – you could do the lunchtime sessions."

"Ha! Yeah—in my 'spare' time. Not likely. When did you come down?" Mick asked, disguising his investigation in casual conversation.

"Friday afternoon. I thought I'd get away from home on the anniversary. Marion and I used to come here for a getaway sometimes. It was our special place. Memories, you know. I always felt peaceful and relaxed here. I thought that down here, I could get some peace to concentrate on my writing. It didn't work—I kept feeling Marion should be here, and her absence was very disturbing. I got angry and sad and… fuck…. I don't know what…. lost, I suppose. Haven't written a word yet."

"What are you writing?"

"Another murder mystery. The usual whodunnit thing."

"What's it about?"

"When I've finished, I'll know. It's been hard to focus on it this weekend."

"You look tired, Dave."

"I am. I didn't sleep much last night. Remembering that night last year. I don't mind telling you, Mick, I cried most of the night. It's just so fucking unfair! My gut was churning at the thought of how senseless it is. And that scumbag got away with it…. or maybe he didn't, after all. I bet he's got no shortage of enemies that would like him off the scene. Anyway, I got up and went for an early walk on the beach, trying to distract my thoughts. Better than lying awake, seething. But now I feel completely stuffed. I'm going to try to sleep today. The story can wait. Tell me about what happened to Price."

"Well, that's all a mystery at this point. Forensics are combing the area as we speak. Hopefully, some clues will show up. Seems he was stabbed once with a long-bladed knife – probably a kitchen knife, but the post-mortem will tell us more. The killer must have been strong and skilled, his hands were bound behind his back with giant zip ties and his ankles as well."

"Sounds like they didn't want him running away." David added.

The detective got back to business. "You say you came down Friday afternoon. Did anyone see you on Friday?"

"The staff at the supermarket in Swansea. I got supplies before heading down here. And Mrs. Jones. She owns the cottage. I collected the keys from her about 4.15, maybe 4.30. Around about then. If I knew I was going to have to remember it, I would have paid more attention. She lives in the house down the road."

"And you've been here ever since?"

David chuckled. "Don't you mean; *where were you on the night of the 13th?*"

"Something like that." David handed Mick his coffee. "You know the drill, Dave. Anyway, at this point, you're our only suspect."

"Can't you trace someone's movements from their phone?"

"Yes, if we have to. It takes a bit of time to get the info from the phone company."

"Well, trace me, and you'll see where I've been. You've got my number."

"I've got my people working on that already. We need to cover off on any options."

"Of course."

"So, last night?"

"I bet Mrs. J. could tell you. She's like Mrs. Kravitz from 'Bewitched.' I was up till about 10.30, 11.00 maybe. I sent a text message to Judy before I went to bed. Hang on a sec; I can check."

David fetched out his phone. "Yes, here it is - 10.43; I sent the message. Shit, that reminds me. I said I'd call her this morning.

She will be upset today, as well. I invited her to come down here for the weekend, but she and James had a dinner date on Saturday night with their friends Janice and Bill Carruthers. And she doesn't like to be away from the kids. She had her second last year, and they called him David. I was touched. But it's tragic Marion never got to meet him. I had better call her shortly."

Mick sipped his steaming coffee. "Do you know anything about Price that might help? Like, I know you think he killed Marion, so have you dug up any dirt on him – any ideas as to who would want him dead – besides you, of course?"

"Not really. I'm not that interested. Just the thought of that prick makes me sick. I've tried to put him out of my mind." David sipped his tea and stared at the floor. "That mate of his – Ogden – he's a nasty piece of work. Those fuckers were as thick as thieves. Perhaps you can ask him."

"We will. But the word is they are not quite so chummy as they used to be. Apparently had a falling out over something—a woman, I think."

"Yeah, I heard all about it from Barry at the White Horse. Price shagged Ogden's bird in the carpark. He thought they were in a dark corner, but those night vision security cameras are amazing. Barry kept the footage for his own entertainment. But John McInerny was well pissed off when he found out that he shagged her over the bonnet of his XJ. Not half as pissed off as Ogden was though, he was livid."

"I heard the same, but didn't know about Dr. McInerny's Jag. I can just imagine his face when he found out. But certainly, Ogden was well mad at Price."

"Enough to kill him?"

"Who could know? Anyway, we'll check him out." Mick finished his coffee and leaned back on the couch. "So, you have been here since Friday?"

David chuckled again. "Do you think I might have driven all the way down here on Friday and then driven back on Saturday, killed Price mysteriously at the same place he killed Marion, then driven back here again. Possible – but a bit of a long shot. Not a scenario my readers would believe. Anyway, my car hasn't moved since I got here. Ask Mrs. J.—Gwen Jones. She doesn't miss a thing like I said."

"I will," Mick announced, standing up. "Thanks for the coffee, Dave. I'll contact you if I need anything else."

Mick looked at David for a moment. "You look buggered, Dave. Are you sure you are ok?"

"Yeah. I'll be fine. I just haven't slept, that's all. Well, that's not all, really. I feel sad and angry and bloody frustrated that Marion is not here anymore. Fuck, it tightens my guts, sometimes."

"Take it easy, mate. Call Judy. Get some rest. Tomorrow is a new day. Those grandkids of yours will be glad to have you around for a long time yet."

"Thanks, Mick. Don't worry. I'm not about to do anything stupid. Anyway, how are you coping? You look tired yourself. How's Karen and your kids."

"I tell you, Dave, this job gets to me sometimes. Too many mysteries, lies, dead ends. Karen wants me to take a break. Our eldest, Jordie, is an engineer, you know that – you taught him at Kings. He's taken a job on a Hyrdo project in Australia. I would love to go down there and check it out."

"Make it happen, Mick. You only live once."

Judd got up to collect his coat. "Now, there's a blast from the past!" He said, pointing to the stereo unit, which included a turntable and cassette player.

"I'll say," David replied. "But I tell you what. I've kept all my vinyls and cassettes from the 70s and 80s. I usually bring a few up with me to play. Even though I've got one of those new-fangled Bluetooth things, there are some old favourites you just can't get on Spotify. This old girl still sounds great. I begged Mrs. J to leave it here – just for me."

Judd observed the record on the turntable. "Classic! Dark Side of The Moon!"

"Yeah. Gave it a spin last night. I hope it wasn't too loud for Mrs. J. I like it loud. Get the full effect. It takes me to another place and time. A happy place."

"I get that. I know exactly what you mean." Judd said, heading for the door. "Anyway, it looks like you're a long shot for Price's murderer. I had better get back and do some chasing."

"Good luck, Mick. Anyway, today, I am going to try to get some sleep. I'm a bit annoyed, now – there I was tossing and turning and churning all night over that prick getting away with murder, and all that time he was dead. But I guess if I'd known, I would have been up all night celebrating. Thanks, Mick, for the great news." David smiled. "You know what, Mick? You have given me a great idea for a crime story. Let me think about that. I reckon there is a real curly yarn in that. Something for later."

"I look forward to reading it, Dave," Mick said politely as he donned his coat and headed out to his car. The rain had eased. David watched through the window as he drove to Mrs. J's and went to the door. Sitting down on the sofa, he thought, *that went well. I had better ring Jude.*

****

Chief inspector Michael Judd knocked on the door of the old farmhouse. A short, bespeckled woman with curly grey hair answered the door, wiping wet hands on her apron.

"Mrs. Jones? Chief inspector Michael Judd." Said Mick, flashing his badge. "May I come in?"

"Yes certainly, what is this about?"

"Just a few quick questions. I'm investigating an incident in Gloucester last night."

"Gloucester?! What has that got to do with me?"

"Your guest in the cottage—David Croswell. When did he arrive?"

"Friday afternoon, around 4.25. he came and collected the keys from me."

"And he has been here ever since?"

"Yes. As far as I can tell, he hasn't gone anywhere apart from getting the Saturday paper from the shop in Port. He usually rides the bike into Port on a Saturday morning to get the local paper - if the weather's fine. His car hasn't moved since he arrived. I can see the whole cottage from here. I saw the living room lights on until about 10.30 or 11. Then he goes to bed."

"How can you tell?"

"The bedroom light goes on for a few minutes, then off."

"Well, you certainly keep a close eye on things."

"Yes, well, since my husband passed, I like to know what's happening around the place."

"And last night. Did you see anything unusual?"

"No. I think David was up until about 11. I heard his music playing—Pink Floyd - Dark Side of The Moon. I'd know it anywhere. It was one of my favourites. Tom, my late husband, and I would play it often."

"I see. Did he play the whole album?"

"Yes, absolutely. From 'Speak to Me' to 'Eclipse.' The whole thing."

"You certainly know it well. What time was that?"

"About 9.30, I suppose, he started. All lights were out by about 11. Maybe a little earlier. I turned in at around 11.15."

"And did you see David at all yesterday?"

"He was sitting on the front porch with the paper when I was heading into Swansea to do some shopping and have lunch with my friends Mabel and Joan. We're all widows now, we meet every Saturday at 1.00 – usually at the Slug and Lettuce – but sometimes we go to the P'n'P."

"The P'n'P?"

"Pitcher and Piano – good pub meals. The 3 widows club we call ourselves. It's been a regular thing for over 4 years now. Anyway, I stopped to ask him if he wanted me to get him anything. He said he was right for everything and said he was going to have a sleep in the afternoon - he didn't sleep well Friday night, he said."

"What time was that?"

"Must have been about 12.40. I don't like to keep those cranky old birds waiting. I drove straight home when I came back – about 4.45 - went quietly past his cottage, so I didn't wake him if he was asleep."

"Could David have gone somewhere on the bike while you were away?"

"No, I would have seen the bike tracks in the sand – It wasn't windy. If he'd gone on the bike I would have known."

"Thank you, Mrs. Jones. Do you know David well?"

"Not really. He comes down for a few days or a week every now and then—four or five times a year. He and Marion used to come......... until............... you know. He hasn't been here since it happened – until this weekend."

"Yes, I know. Nasty business. Thank you, I must be off now."

"I hope I have been some help. But I don't know anything about Gloucester – except David lives near there."

"You have been most helpful. Thank you, again, Mrs. Jones."

"Everyone calls me Mrs. J."

"Thank you, Mrs. J."

The detective collected his coat and braced himself against the wind as Gwen opened the door for him.

"Good day, Mrs. J."

As he drove back along the A465, Inspector Judd had much to ponder. His only suspect at this point appeared to have a rock-solid alibi. And he had known David for some time, and he didn't fit for a murderer. But the coincidence of the place and date was too much to ignore. The only other person that may have a connection with that place and date was William Ogden. That would be his next point of call. Hopefully, his team would have some information from Price's phone company by now to shed some light on his final movements. Why was he at the place Marion was killed, exactly one year later? It was a mystery, but far too much of a coincidence to discount a connection with David Croswell – or even Ogden. He still believed he had a hand in Marion's murder. There just had to be some connection.

Part 3. Proof

At Gloucester CID HQ, the investigation team was piecing together information about Price's final days and hours.

Constable Jenny Farmer sat staring into her computer screen, her tight-wave black hair tied back in a bun. Her West-Indian features reflected on the screen. She had been in touch with the phone companies and had traced both Price's and Croswell's phones for the past 48 hours. She had just received the information and pressed 'Print' when Judd arrived back at the station. Judd walked purposefully into the office, where a handful of officers sat at desks covered with files, with just enough space for a keyboard and computer screen.

"Anything from the phone companies, Jen?" he said as he entered.

"Yes, just got it. Price had a series of text messages from a contact in the days before his demise. They had arranged to meet at 'the place' after 9 pm before heading to the White Horse Inn for a drink."

"That could be Ogden, William Ogden?"

"Possibly. We are looking into it. If we can find Price's phone, that will tell us a lot more."

"What about Ogden's phone?"

"We don't know his number or provider. He must go prepaid."

"Alright, then, Jen, what else do we know about Price's movements?"

Jen looked back at her printout. "It appears that Price had been at home in Highnam all afternoon until 8.37. He then travelled to Maisemore and parked on The Rudge at the end of the path. He then walked to the place his body was found, arriving at 8.52. We know he His phone went off at 9.17. No movement after that."

"Not surprising, considering that he was dead." Judd offered. "Obviously, whoever killed him must have taken his phone and turned it off so it couldn't be traced. What about Croswell?"

Jennifer looked at her printout again. "Croswell left home at 1.15 on the 12th May and travelled along the A465 to Swansea, stopped briefly at a petrol station, and arrived at the town at 3.47. He spent 26 minutes in the town centre before driving out to Port Talbot and to the cottage. Did some shopping, I suppose. On Saturday morning he went into Port Talbot and returned to the cottage about 8.37. Doesn't look like he's gone anywhere since. They've given us a map showing his movements if you want."

"That's pretty much exactly what he told me." Judd scratched his chin. "And his landlady corroborated it. Anything else? Calls, messages in the past 48 hours?"

"It looks like he doesn't use his phone much," Jen continued. He made a call to a London number on Thursday for three and a half minutes. Turns out that the call was directed to his publisher. He received a call from his daughter, Judy, at 11.16 on Friday. He sent a text message to Judy at 10.43 pm last night."

"Do we know where the text message was sent from?"

Jenny studied her printout again. "Here it is - originated from tower 3856 – Swansea east.

"Thanks, Jen." Judd pondered his next move.

"Anything on the boot-prints, Ewen?" Judd asked, directing his question to a ginger-headed young detective in an ill-fitting brown suit.

"There are a number of different ones in the area. But the prints forensics think may belong to the killer are size 10, Doc Martens. Very popular with tradesmen. There would be hundreds of them out there."

"Anything distinctive about these?"

"Well, yes. The middle of the soles under the arches are worn and have a lot of small chips."

"Meaning?"

"Meaning that the wearer probably rides a bicycle or climbs a lot of ladders – or both. The pedals wear away at the arch of the soles – like the rungs of a ladder would as well."

"Could we identify the boots from the prints at the crime scene?"

"Maybe. But there are other boot prints there as well. From people walking along the track. Other size 10 Doc Martens, even. It could be a long shot to prove the boots that made the prints belonged to the killer. And if we don't find the matching boots shortly, the markings will change if they keep being used on a bicycle."

"Yes. But if we could find the matching boots, they might hold some other clues." Judd pondered this and then remembered that he saw a pair of Doc Martens on Croswell's doorstep.

Judd, accompanied by Jennifer Farmer, knocked loudly on Ogden's door. Four uniformed officers waited behind.

An unshaven, bleary-eyed Ogden opened the door in a dirty white singlet and track pants. "Oh, it's the Filf. What do you want, now?"

"We have a warrant to search these premises."

"Fuck! Really? What for?"

"Can we come in?"

"Well, I don't have any fucking choice, do I, but I haven't prepared for guests - if you know what I mean."

Inside the flat was a mess. A tattered 3-seater couch faced a TV in a tiny living room. The coffee table between was adorned with a few empty pizza boxes, several coffee mugs, a bong, and other items difficult to identify at first glance. There was a stale stench combining mould, tobacco, and marijuana in the air.

The uniforms started searching the rooms.

"If you tell me what you're looking for, I can tell you where to find it!" Ogden shouted up the stairs.

"Fuckers have no respect for a person's property," Ogden said to Judd as he plonked himself on the couch. "Sit down, darling, make yourself at home." He said to Farmer.

"Thank you, but I'd rather stand, thanks."

Judd got to the point. "Where were you last night between 9 and 11 pm?"

"Here. The football was on. After that finished, I had a bong and watched some crap movie until I fell asleep. If you want to do me for possession, the stash is in the kitchen drawer, bottom right."

"We're not interested in your stash. This is a murder investigation."

Ogden's eyes opened up, and he sat himself more upright on the couch. "Murder?! Fuck! Who's copped it?"

"Daniel Price. His body was found by the lake this morning."

"Price?! Jesus Christ! We used to be mates until he shagged my missus. Filthy slag she was. Would fuck anyone when she got pissed. Fucken Price should've had more respect for me—told her to fuck off. She showed him her tits in the pub, right in front of everyone. I pissed off home, and Price shagged her in the carpark—over the bonnet of some fucker's Jag - the dirty prick. She could have done him in—wouldn't put anything past the slut, after what she did to me."

Jennifer was clearly uncomfortable with his language.

"Sorry, darling, just calling it as I see it. I bet you're not the type to shag your boyfriend's mate. No, straight down the line, you'd be. Hey, darlin' ow'd you like to spend the night on my boat?"

"As if, Where's your boat?"

"You're lookin' at it." Ogden chuckled.

Unperturbed by Ogden's cheap joke at Jen's expense, Judd continued. "Can anyone corroborate your alibi?"

Ogden thought for a moment. "Only Mrs. Palmer and 'er five daughters." He chuckled.

"Who are they?" Jenifer asked.

"Never mind that," Judd interjected, "I'll explain later."

Just then, a uniformed officer poked his head around the corner, " Sir. You had better look at this."

They proceeded to the back door of the flat, followed by Ogden. A pair of Doc Martens work boots were on the back doorstep.

"Are these your boots?"

"Looks like 'em."

"We need to take them for evidence."

"Why? Are you saying I killed Price?"

"Not yet. But they could either incriminate or clear you. Do you have a bicycle?"

"Yes, in the shed. Have to fucken ride everywhere since you fuckers took my licence. But it's got a flat. So, now I'm on shank's pony. 'Ang about, there's something odd about those boots. I always take them off with the toes facing the wall, but they're facing the other way. Have you moved them?"

"No, not touched them." The officer said.

"That's strange. I'm sure I left them toes to the wall."

"We will need to confiscate your phone too. Can I have it, please?" Judd ordered.

"That's another odd thing," Ogden said. "I lost my phone on Wednesday night at the pub or somewhere. Couldn't find it when I got home. Then this morning, when I got up, there it was by the front door. It couldn't have been there all along. I would have seen it, surely. Not that I use the front door much—usually go out the back to the alley. But I did come in the front door Wednesday night. Could've dropped it, I s'pose. Fucken bike had a flat, so I caught a lift. Jock McKenzie dropped me home. Maybe someone found it and put it through the letter flap. But how would they

43

know it was mine?" Ogden thought a moment. "Of course! I stash a couple of my cards under the cover. They could have got my details from there. It's not much fucken use to me in the day, anyway. Most sites wouldn't let you have your phone on you. Fucken safety Nazis. You can get kicked off if they see you on your phone on the site. Sometimes I leave the bloody thing home anyway, doesn't matter shit, no fucker ever calls me."

Ogden pulled the phone from his pocket and handed it to Judd. "Here. Battery's flat. You'll have to charge it first."

Judd placed the phone carefully in an evidence bag. "What's your passcode?"

"1-2-3-4"

The officers left with a few bags of evidence- boots, phone, dirty clothes, and some other items.

"When will I get my boots and phone back? I need them for work tomorrow."

"As soon as forensics are finished with them. I suggest that you get some replacements in the meantime." Judd answered. "It could be a while."

"Fucken Filf!" Ogden slammed the door.

On the way back to the station, Judd was in deep thought as Jennifer drove. "What do you make of that, sir?" She asked.

Judd looked blankly out the window. "It is very odd. Ogden did not at all behave like someone that has just committed a murder. He wasn't trying to hide anything. But the boots, bicycle...... I don't know. That comment about his boots being the wrong way round, the missing phone that mysteriously turns up. Something is amiss here. But there is certainly no love lost between him and Price. Enough to kill him? I'm not feeling that. Seems he blamed the girlfriend more than Price. And would he have the smarts to take Price's phone after he killed him and turn it off so it couldn't be traced? Unlikely, but possible. In the meantime, we'll keep an eye on Ogden—see if he does anything rash."

There was a lingering thought in his mind. *What if Ogden was being set up? What if someone wanted to make it look like he killed Price? Who would know how to do this and would want to? Only one name came to mind—Crime writer David Croswell. But he had a rock-solid alibi. Perhaps he hired a killer. But they are expensive. He would know we could track down any payment. He would be unlikely to have access to enough cash to pay a killer. Who else would want Price dead? That would be an interesting question. He sounds like the sort of person who would accumulate enemies.*

Back at Gloucester CID, Judd leaned back in his office chair, looking at the ceiling. *Why don't the cleaners ever get rid of the cobwebs? They never look up. Only ever look down.* There was a knock on his open door. It was Jen Farmer.

"Jen. What have you got?"

"The ex-girlfriend—Sharon. Broke up with Price a couple of months ago and moved to Essex. I don't think she's in the picture."

"Good. What else?"

"Ogden's phone. We've charged and opened it. Now that we know his number and service provider, we can get a trace on it."

"How long will that take?"

"A day or two. Anyway, the messages to Price came from his phone. Thursday, Friday, and Saturday."

"The days he says his phone was 'missing'. Interesting. So, what have we got?"

"Thursday 8.15 pm: 'Been having nightmares that the truth will come out. Not saying anything, are u?'

Price replies: 'All good, my end.'

Ogden replies: 'Just that a bloke on the site said something that worried me. Said u were spouting shit in the pub about it."

Friday 10:07 am: 'Talked to my mate on site again today. Sed u was saying how u got away with it - when u was pissed.'

Price replies: 'Bullshit Said fuck all. U keep your trap shut. That stupid cow shouldn't have been walking out there at night'.

Ogden Replies: 'No prob from me, but you say all sorts of shit when ur pissed. Remember, that's how you got us in the shit over this in the first place.'

Price replies: 'Yeah, fair nuff.'

Ogden replies: 'M8, forget about that shit with Sharon. She dumped u anyway. I don't want any shit between us that might let the cat out of the bag, or we'll both go down. Can I meet u tomorrow night at the place? By the lake, u know where. Where it happened, no one will see us there. Talk things over. We had fun in the old days let's get over this shit and get back to being m8s.'

Price replies: 'ok, but it has to be 9 after the football.'

Ogden replies: 'All good, maybe we could go for a drink at the white Horse after.'

Price replies: 'Ok'

Then on Saturday at 6.13 pm: 'U good for 9? Let's get our story str8, and we'll have a drink, ok?'

Price replies: 'OK, I'll be there.'

Mick Judd thought about the messages "As far as I'm concerned, that's proof that they committed the Croswell murder, but it wouldn't stand up in court without anything else to support it. It's all a bit odd. They arrange a meeting, seemingly in good faith— with a bit of tension, then, Price gets hog-tied and stabbed. What do you see as wrong with this picture, Jen?"

"Well, it didn't appear to me that Ogden had forgiven Price when we talked to him today. And if he did want to kill Price, why that day and place? It would surely only draw attention to his possible guilt in the Croswell case. It doesn't make sense to me. There must be something else at play here. But if he did intend to kill Price, he would pretend to be all good with him so he would meet him there."

"There's always something else, Jen. We need to find the murder weapon. That may give us some more clues. In the meantime, can you trace where the messages were sent from and where that phone's been? And take the phone to that linguistics nutter at the Uni. What's his name…? Dr…….. fucken………. Morris… that's it, Dr. Paul Morris. I want to know if there are any differences in these latest messages from the previous ones."

"Yes, Gov."

"Put some pressure on the phone company. I need to know where his phone has been. It might clear up the question of whether his phone was missing or not. And go up to Maisemore, to the White Horse Inn. Publican's name is Barry. Download a copy of his security camera record from Saturday night. See who was around."

"Gov."

****

48

William Ogden went to his tiny backyard shed to fix the flat tyre on his bicycle. He would need it in the morning to ride into Gloucester to get some new boots and a phone. "Fuck those coppers!" he said aloud.

He removed the nuts from the front wheel and put them on the floor. Turning around in the tight space, he knocked one of the nuts under the old cupboard that stored various garden chemicals and tools. "Fuck!" He reached under the cupboard to find the nut, when his hand felt something else there. Curious, he pulled it out. A long-bladed kitchen knife came into view, which he had pulled out by the handle. Dried blood covered the blade, the handle, and was now on his hand. It soon dawned on him what it was. This was the knife that killed Price. And now it had his fingerprints on it. Realising what this would mean if the police found it, he panicked. He grabbed a rag he used to wipe his hands on and wiped the handle to remove any prints, then he wrapped the knife in the rag. *Got to get rid of it, fast. But where? Throw it in the river? No, someone might see him. Bury it in the forest? That would work. There is a big patch of forest a few miles up the road near Hartpury. No one goes there much.*

Ogden hastily repaired his bike and set off towards Hartpury, heat thumping, with the wrapped knife and a garden trowel in his backpack. The sun was low in the sky. 15 minutes later, he turned off the main road into Hiam's Lane. He dismounted where the woods met the road and concealed the bike in the underbrush. He pushed into the forest for 5 minutes or so and then dug a hole about a foot and a half deep near the roots of an old oak tree. He buried the knife, still wrapped in the rag, and brushed leaves and debris over the diggings. Satisfied that it was never going to be found, he returned to his bike and headed home, arriving as the sun set over the hills.

****

The following Tuesday morning, Chief Inspector Judd arrived at his office.

"Forensics are in," Jennifer said as he entered.

"And?" Judd asked, hanging up his coat.

"The boots from Ogden's place are a positive match for the prints at the crime scene."

"Great! What else?"

"There are traces of Price's blood on his phone."

"That's very interesting. Bring him in."

"I've got Uniform on to it. But we're having trouble finding him. We can't trace him because we've got his phone. I've already had some clown downstairs tell me he is in the station. He works as a casual labourer. He could be anywhere in the area."

"Well, pick him up when he comes home."

"And hold him overnight?"

"Just find him, for fuck's sake!!"

"Yes, sir."

"Any joy on the murder weapon?"

"No, sir. Uniform will do another scan of the area. They have been doing magnetic fishing in the lake nearby to find the knife, but no luck."

"That's useless if it was a good stainless-steel knife. The magnet won't pick it up."

"Sir."

"How did you get on at the White Horse?"

"Good. Barry was very helpful. He wanted to show me the Price and Sharon footage, but I declined the offer. Neither Price nor Ogden, nor Croswell were in the bar Saturday night. I've got the security camera file. I haven't looked at it yet. The files are overwritten every four days or so, so we were lucky he still had it. It only shows the carpark out front, though."

"Ok. Take some time to look at it today. There might be something on it that helps us."

"Ewen! Have we heard back from the pathologist?"

"Yes, Gov. I've got the report here. 'Severe bruising to the chest consistent with impact from a boot. Bruising to left abdomen. Lacerations to wrists and ankles from the zip ties.'"

"And the cause of death?"

"'Single stab wound to the chest – through the heart.' Death would have been pretty quick."

"Anything about the murder weapon that could help us find it?"

"Well, Interestingly, the report says that the blade was double-sided. So, not a standard kitchen knife. More like a throwing knife, but thinner."

'See if you can find anyone in the area that sells knives like that. Although, these days, everyone buys stuff online, so it could have come from anywhere."

"Yes, Gov."

Later that day, Jen Farmer called Judd to her computer, where she had been perusing the video from the White Horse.

"Have a look at this, Sir. Time is 9.27. Who does that look like, crossing the carpark?"

"Looks like Ogden to me. Just run it through again."

They both watched intently. Suddenly Judd said, "Stop there!"

The figure crossing the carpark had momentarily looked in the direction of the camera. "Ogden! And he said he was home. Not much doubt now, I reckon."

Judd considered his strategy. Hey Jen, Keep this video under wraps for now. We'll see how it matches up to his phone trace when we get it. Might keep it in the gun for later, or leave it for something to surprise him with in court."

A few hours later, Farmer received an email from the phone company with the details of the phone's movements since the previous Wednesday. She knocked on Judd's door.

"Gov, have a look at this. Ogden's phone. It was off all day Wednesday until 4.30. Then on until 6.49 pm at the Dick Whittington Hotel. Then its goes off. It is only switched on for the brief periods that the messages are sent – until 8.49 Saturday night. It goes from Ogden's home, up Old Road to the track where Price was killed. Then 12 minutes later, it goes to The Rudge, down past the White Horse Inn and back to Ogden's home."

"Very Interesting. And what about the time it crosses the carpark? How does that match up to Barry's CCTV?"

"Exactly. His phone crosses the carpark the same time he does. He can't talk his way out of that!"

"No. But something else I want you to check, Jen. Plot all the places the phone was when the messages were sent and check them against Ogden's movements. "

53

"Will do, Sir." Farmer replied, with some doubts as to why they needed any more convincing of his guilt.

****

At 6 am the following morning, Ogden was brought in. In Interview Room 1, Michael Judd and Jennifer Farmer sat opposite a perplexed-looking Ogden and his assigned lawyer. He was unshaven and his hair was bestraggled and dirty. He wasn't smelling particularly fresh either.

Judd led the interview. On the table were two evidence bags—one with a pair of boots and one with a phone.

"Now, William, there have been some developments in our enquiries. The boots found at your back door, that you say are yours, match the boot prints found at the scene of Price's murder."

"So, what? Hundreds of blokes wear Doc Martens."

"Yes, but yours are specifically worn a certain way from your bicycle pedals, and that is what matches the prints at the scene."

"Fucking impossible! I wasn't there! I told you I was home all night!"

"Yes. But there is the matter of the phone messages you sent to Price."

"What are you talking about? I never messaged that cunt!"

"Control your language, please, Mr. Ogden. We have four messages sent from your phone on Thursday 11th May to Saturday 13th May."

"I told you. I lost my phone on Wednesday. Then it turned up on Sunday morning. I didn't message anyone. I didn't have my phone!"

"Well, there's another thing. There are traces of Price's blood on your phone. Can you explain that?"

"Of course, I can't! I didn't have my phone! Whoever did have must have killed Price! Fucking Hell! I'm being stitched up here."

Ogden considered whether it would help to fess up about the knife. But decided against it.

"William Ogden, we are arresting you on suspicion of the murder of Daniel Price. You will be remanded in custody pending bail application."

"This is Bullshit! I'm being fitted up. Fuck!"

****

Ogden lay on the hard bed, thinking things over. *Fucking Price! Why the fuck did he have to club that woman? Could have just left her alone and walked home. The stupid prick always had to be the big man. Treats women like shit. No fucking wonder someone knocked him off........ 'Keep your trap shut, and we'll be right,' he said. I should have grassed on the cunt. But he would have said I*

55

did it—his word against mine.... That's the sort of prick he is.... was. 'She'll come round in a minute,' he said... fucking killed her, the dickhead. Fuck, this is a mess.... Now they think I killed him. Some bastard is fitting me up for it. Could be Croswell. What do I do now? Maybe if I tell them about Price clubbing that woman........

The next morning, Ogden sat again in the interview room awaiting further interrogation. Judd and Farmer came in.

Jennifer led the questions. "We have looked back through your phone a little further at conversations with Price. On March 20th, you sent a message: *"Don't fuck with me, remember I know what you did."*

To which he replied: *"Fuck off ur in as deep as me say anything, and ur ded meat. I'll grass you up quick as fuck. One word and ur fucked, mate."*

Would you like to tell us about that?"

"Told you. He shagged my missus."

"Anything more.... what did you mean by *'I know what you did?'*"

Ogden stared at the table. It was time. Price couldn't contradict him now. "That woman.... Croswell.... he fucking killed 'er. Hit her on the head with a tree branch, the stupid cunt. Why the fuck he did it, I don't know. He's always done crazy shit when he gets pissed, goes fucken mental. He pinched the cash out of her purse, and we left her there – just thought she was knocked out, that's all."

Judd stared at the man opposite for a moment to gather his thoughts. "You haven't exactly got a clean record when it comes to violence, yourself. You have done time for GBH. Why should we believe that it wasn't you that hit Marion Croswell, and you that killed Daniel Price?"

"I wised up after 6 months in that shit-hole. That was 3 years ago, I've been clean ever since. Check my record. Fuck getting banged up for doin' somin' stupid. I don't want that shit in my life again."

"So, what happened to sour your friendship with Daniel Price?" Farmer asked.

"When I had a go at him for shagging Sharon, he got all fucken angry, said he'd grass *me* up for doin' that woman over."

"How did you feel about that?"

"Wanted to kill the cunt. Fucken shags my missus, then fucken says he's gonna fucken grass on me for somin' he did? How'd ya reckon I'd fucken feel?"

"Did you kill him?" Jennifer asked, ignoring his swearing.

"No. Just got him out of my life. What did I say in the next message?"

Jen Farmer looked at her notes. "*Tell Sharon from me she's a fucken slag u can keep the bitch fuck off.*"

"Yeah, that's the one. I never contacted him again."

"Until last Thursday," Judd added.

"I told ya. I lost my phone on Wednesday. I didn't send any messages to that slimy piece of shit."

"Yes, you told us. You can see how this looks, William. You have more than one reason to want to kill him, your boots at the scene, his blood on your phone. It's not looking good for you. You've already admitted to lying in court about the Croswell murder. We could go for a retrial on that alone. So why don't you just tell us what you did Saturday night between 9 and 10 pm?"

Ogden leaned forward and looked Judd directly in the eyes. "I told you where I was…...at 'ome. I didn't meet up with Price and kill him, Ok." Ogden leaned back in his chair and crossed his arms. "I'm not saying nothin' more."

"What did you do with the murder weapon?" Jennifer added.

Ogden stared at her with a look of disbelief, then tilted his head back, looking at the ceiling. "For fuck's sake," he muttered, shaking his head.

On Thursday morning, Ogden was granted bail on a £10,000 bond put up by his mother—against the prosecutor's advice. Judd sat in his office, fuming. *'How the fuck can they grant bail when we have so much evidence against him? He'll do a runner, for sure.'*

A young detective knocked on his door.

"Yes, Ewen?"

"Gov, you won't believe what just happened. A woman came in with a knife wrapped in a rag she found up in Hartpury Forest. Her Jack Russell dug it up. I think we may have our murder weapon. I sent it straight to the lab."

"Brilliant! Let me know what they find."

The results came back a few hours later. Blood on the blade was Price's. This was the murder weapon. No prints on the handle, wiped clean. DNA testing of the rag found three sets of DNAs— One was the dog's, another unknown – likely the woman who brought it in; and Ogden's.

"We've definitely got him, now!" Judd said gleefully.

"Bring him in. We'll charge him with Price's murder and wrap this up."

Ogden was back in the Interview room's familiar surroundings when Judd and Farmer came in carrying an evidence bag. They put it on the table in front of Ogden.

Ogden looked at the knife and rag. "Jesus!"

"Do you recognise these items? Judd asked.

"Yes. Can I explain?"

"I'm all ears," Judd replied, leaning back in his chair with a smug grin.

"I found the knife in my shed, under the cupboard. I was trying to get the nut from my bike that rolled under there. Your plods didn't do much of a job searching. They should have found it. I knew straight up what it was. Some fucker is trying to stitch me up. I panicked – knowing the other shit you had on me. So, I wrapped it in a rag and buried it in Hartpury forest where no one would find it…. How the fuck *did* you find it?"

"A Jack Russell dug it up. They're all nose. Are you trying to tell me that you didn't hide the knife in your shed, and you didn't take it straight to Hartpury Forest?"

"I might not be the brightest bulb in the chandelier, but I'm not that fucken stupid. If I'd killed Price with it, I would have just chucked it in the fucken river. Never get found. Anyway, I couldn't have taken it to Hartpury 'til Sunday night coz my bike had a flat. I was fixin' it when I found the knife."

"Very interesting. But I don't think the Jury will swallow it."

"And, perhaps you can explain this." Judd said, putting in front of Ogden the printout of his phone trace showing it leaving his home at 8.49pm, going up Old Road, along the track by the lake, then after 12 minutes, travelling down The Rudge to the motorway and back to his home.

"Well, obviously, whoever killed Danny had my phone!"

"Yes. I agree." Judd concurred, and placed the photo of him crossing the carpark on the table on front of him. "Do you recognise this man? Take note of the time on the photo. 9.27. Exactly the same time that your phone was crossing the carpark. More than a coincidence, wouldn't you agree? And the duffle coat he's wearing – top left- hand button missing – just like the one we took from your home."

"This is bullshit!! I was at home all last Saturday night! My coat was hanging in the hall."

"But that *is* you in the photo, isn't it?" Judd waited as Ogden stared at the photo in disbelief.

"I don't know how the fuck you got that photo, but it wasn't me. I wasn't there."

"I think maybe you need to be more careful about what you put in your bong, Billy. You must have got some nasty shit Saturday night."

"Fucking Hell!! This is a fit-up!"

"You'll face a committal hearing tomorrow, and there will be a date set for your trial. You have the right to engage your own lawyer or use one provided."

Judd Continued. "One more thing. We need you to stand in an identity parade. Our call for witnesses has found a woman who says she saw someone in the area around 9.25, coming down The Rudge, away from where Price was killed."

Ogden stood in a row of 7 men, he was holding a card bearing the number 4.

The woman walked slowly along behind the glass panel, looking at all the faces. "I'm not sure. It was dark and ...."

"Have another look, take your time." Jennifer urged.

"That's him, number 4."

"Are you certain?"

"Yes, number 4."

****

Part 4. Doubts

Back in his office, Judd pondered the situation. He summoned the young detective, Ewen.

"Go to Ogden's place and have a look in his shed out the back. He claims that he found the knife under the cupboard. Get forensics over there to look for traces of blood on the floor. Ask Jen to come in here, please."

"Sir."

Detective Constable Farmer came to the door.

"Yes, Gov?"

"Sit down, close the door."

Judd looked at the young, dark woman opposite him. "What's your ambition in the force, Jen?"

"Well, sir, I want to rise to a higher rank, make Chief Inspector, maybe."

"Right. But why?"

"Well, sir. We work in the pursuit of justice, fighting crime. I want to bring criminals to justice under the law."

"And what is the underlying driver of all that?"

"Well, sir, I suppose it's the truth. Finding the truth, that's it."

"Quite. But, you know, if four people see the same event, you'll get four different versions of the truth. Which one is the actual truth?"

"I don't know, sir."

"The actual truth, Jen, is the version you *choose* to be the truth. All versions are true—it just depends which one you choose. What is the truth for someone may not be so for another."

"What are you getting at, sir?"

"The 'Truth' is not a definitive thing, sometimes. Perhaps it never is. This Price murder, what do you make of it?"

"Open and shut case. We have the perpetrator with more than one motive. We have the evidence, and we have a positive ID to prove that he was lying about staying home that night. And he was heading in a direction away from the murder scene, at a time just after when the murder was committed. All pretty easy, really."

"Exactly. *All pretty easy*. That's exactly what bothers me, Jen. *Too* bloody easy. If you want to be a good detective, you need to look beyond the obvious. Something that Ogden said bothers me about the knife he claims was stashed under his cupboard. '*Your plods should have found it.*' Yes, they should have. Because, just maybe, it was put there for them to find."

"By who?"

"By the real killer."

"Who is?"

"I do not know. But think about it. What if he *didn't* stash the knife under the cupboard and accidentally found it? And why would he take the weapon home? What if his phone *did* get stolen, and he *didn't* send those messages? What if his boots *were* taken by the murderer and put back – the wrong way around? What if the woman is mistaken about who she saw - in the dark? He is still claiming innocence, and we couldn't find any trace of blood or Price's DNA on his clothes. Only his boots. That is very unusual."

"But what about the carpark photo and his phone trace?"

"That is doing my head in. Everything else has a possible alternative explanation, but not that. Maybe I'm getting too old for this job, Jen. Trusting my instincts has led me to many successful convictions, but now my instincts seem to be failing me. My brain feels twisted by the contradiction of what I'm feeling and what I'm seeing."

"So, what now?"

"I need a holiday."

"No, I mean with Ogden."

"Tricky. I can't drop the charge against Ogden, given how much evidence against him we have. I can't delay the trial on the basis of my doubts. I can't refuse to hand over the evidence to the prosecutor. The Super would have my guts for garters. The wheels are in motion now. Unless we find anything to the contrary, Ogden is going down for it. And you know, he might just actually be guilty, after all. I think he never stopped hating Price's guts since the Sharon incident and Price threatening him. He could well have been very concerned that Price would grass on him for the Croswell murder. 'Dead men tell no tales', you know. Either way, the Superintendent is not going to give us any more time or resources now that the case is solved."

"Can we keep it under wraps? A secret investigation."

"Yes, to a degree. But there's also the moral question. I am absolutely certain that Price killed Marion Croswell. And Ogden was there and lied to protect his mate from going down for it. Now, the murderer - Price is dead, and it looks like his protector, Ogden, will take the rap. Kinda moral justice, isn't it?"

"Poetic."

"Yes, that's what David Croswell said. 'Poetic Justice'."

"Do you think *he* did it – Croswell - killed Price and set Ogden up? He certainly had plenty of motive."

"It just feels incredibly unlikely. He appeared to be genuinely surprised, even if overjoyed, by the news of Price's murder. A 58-year-old writer, ex-teacher with no history of any violence or any crime. He campaigned against any violent form of punishment when he was a teacher. The man is a total law-abiding passivist. He's never so much as got a parking ticket. So, he takes on and murders a fit 28-year-old nut-job with a violent history as long as your arm? I can't see it. Karate or no karate. Anyway, he has a rock-solid alibi that he was 75 miles away at the time of the murder. It's never going to fly. But he does have a motive. And...... the day, the place...... even about the same time. I just don't know what to think about that."

"Should we have another chat with Croswell?"

"Sure – but on what grounds? What tangible *anything* have we got to suspect him? Sweet Fanny Adams! What am I going to ask him? Hey Dave, did you kill Daniel Price? Is he going to say, 'Yeah, it was me'? Not likely. But I'll talk to him anyway, see how he reacts."

"What about the daughter, Sir? Judy. She probably had as much motive as her father."

"Yes, I've thought about her. But it doesn't feel likely. A young mother with a toddler and a new baby, a qualified lawyer. Married to a doctor. I've come across a lot of different murderers in my career, and she's about as far away from the profile of a cold-blooded killer as you can get without being a Buddhist Monk. Feel free to check her out if you wish, but I think you'd be chasing shadows. Apparently, she was at dinner with friends Janice and Bill Carruthers on Saturday night. Check out her alibi, just to be sure."

I little later, Ewen called Judd. "There's a phone under the cupboard, Gov., and some traces of blood. Forensics are dealing with it now."

"Good work, Ewen. Come back now."

Another piece of evidence left for us to find, perhaps? Judd thought as he finished the call.

The forensics report on the phone confirmed that it was Price's phone. It had traces of his blood on it, but no fingerprints other than his. The messages to and from Ogden's phone were there.

Ewen brought Price's phone into Judd's office. Gov, you've got to see this. I am stuffed if I know what's going on here."

Ewen took the phone from the evidence bag, opened the photos app, and selected the last item, a video. They all watched, awestruck, as Price confessed to killing Marion Croswell.

"What in Hell!?" Judd exclaimed.

"Interesting thing is," Ewen continued, "The time is 9.17 pm on the 13th May. Just before he was killed."

"That is very strange," Judd mused. 'Very strange indeed. Why would his killer get him to record a confession of the Croswell murder?"

"Well," Jennifer started, "If it *was* Ogden, he would want to make sure that *he* never went down for the Croswell murder."

"Maybe," Judd replied, "but that would also put him in the frame for Price's murder. What if it was someone else wanting to solve the mystery of Marion's murder?"

"Yes, but why kill him?" Ewen added. "Why not turn him over to police after he got the confession?"

"A couple of things come to mind," Judd explained. "Firstly, Price's lawyer would claim that the confession was made under duress, and it wouldn't be admissible evidence. Secondly, Price would be able to identify his assailant, and they would be in serious likelihood of being charged with a number of offenses – deprivation of liberty, etc. Remember the old western movies: 'dead men tell no tales'."

"What about David Croswell?" Jen asked. "He would want Price dead and would want to hear Price admit to Marion's murder."

"And so would his daughter. Unfortunately, they both have watertight alibis."

****

Judd called Croswell's number on Friday morning. "Hello, Dave – are you back from the coast yet?"

"Yeah, got back yesterday."

"Are you around tomorrow morning? I'll come over."

"Should be here all day. Drop-in anytime."

"Around 10, I'd say."

"Perfect."

****

Mid-morning Saturday, Michael Judd knocked on the front door of David's house.

"Mick!" David said when he opened the door. "Working weekends now?"

"Let's call it a social call."

"Come on, Mick. I know there's no such thing in your game. Come and have a drink. Coffee?"

"Got anything stronger?"

"Beer? Wine? Scotch?"

"Beer."

"Take a seat, Mick. I'll fetch a couple of beers."

David returned shortly with two bottles of ale.

"Cheers." He said, handing one to Judd.

"Yeah. Thought I'd drop by and see how you were. You looked like crap when I saw you last."

"Thanks, Mick. I got better. I stayed a few extra days down there. Got a bit of writing in. Somehow, knowing Price was dead made me feel a lot better than I'd felt for a year. Some sort of closure, I suppose. It's a pity though, that he never paid for killing Marion."

"Perhaps he has now."

"What do you mean?"

"Well, perhaps someone who believed Price killed Marion thought they'd settle the score."

The hint in Judd's statement was not lost on David. "I heard on the news that Ogden had been charged with his murder. Was *he* settling a score?"

Judd considered telling David about Price's video confession of Marion's murder, but thought better of it. "Maybe. Maybe it was someone else."

"How does that work if you've charged Ogden already? You must have enough evidence to charge him."

"We have. More than enough. That's the problem. In my 32 years in the job, I've never seen so much compelling evidence of someone's guilt coming so easily. It doesn't feel right."

"Perhaps you should just go with it, celebrate an easy win."

Mick Judd paused to think for a moment. "I'll tell you something, Dave, that I haven't told anyone before." Judd leaned forward in his seat, as if telling a secret. "When I first made detective, I was all keen and gung-ho, and we got a conviction against a bloke for GBH. Took a lot of witness statements, forensics, and stuff. But the witness statements did the job. I was really chuffed when the 'Guilty' verdict came down. The Super took me for a drink, and it was a great day in my career. I felt real cocky, you know. Got a promotion on the back of it. A couple of years later, I find out it was all bullshit. People lied in their statements and fitted the bloke up for it, so their mate who did it went free. You know what the problem was? I wanted to get a result so bad that I believed the bullshit. There was evidence there that the bloke didn't do it. But I ignored it. Just saw what I wanted to see. That has haunted me ever since. I promised myself that I'd never again put someone away for something they didn't do. So, this Price case...... all the evidence against Ogden falls in our lap. Now I'm asking myself, *'What am I not seeing here?'"*

David could sense where he was going with this. "Geez, Mick, I don't know. Marion was really popular around the village. And you know what the talk was – about Price and Ogden—a lot of people thought they did it – you and I included. A lot of people were pissed off that they both walked. Do you think someone has done this – killed Price for Marion and fitted up Ogden?"

"That's what's bugging me. It's possible. Way possible. Ogden hasn't confessed, still claims he's innocent." Judd put his empty bottle on the coffee table.

"I don't envy you, Mick. I make up these yarns about crimes and cops—it's all fantasy for me. But you are right in there – it's real. Another beer?"

"No, Dave, I'd better go. Karen gets on my case if I'm out all day on the weekend. I told her I was going to the hardware for some garden tools. I was just wondering though…... you went to Amsterdam in March—what was that about?"

"Caught up with an old school chum. They had been pestering me for months to come over. I caught the train down to Paris for a few days, and I wanted to do a bit of on-the-ground research for my new story. So glad I went over. It really gave me some great space from home to get a clearer perspective on life without Marion. George is an IT guru, but it's his attitude to life that's so refreshing. And Eve makes the best cakes in the world!"

"I see. Well, I had better be off." Judd stood up.

"So, what's the deal with Ogden—I suppose he'll be in court shortly."

"July 27th."

"Ok. See you later, Mick. Thanks for dropping by."

"Yeah. Thanks for the beer. Cheers Dave."

****

"How did you get on with Croswell?" Jen Farmer asked Mick when he arrived Monday morning.

"If he is in any way connected to Price's murder, he is a fantastic liar. There was not a hint in his face or anything that suggested he knew anything about it. I've been reading people's body language and faces for 30 years. I saw nothing. You know, you look for that slight blush or loss of colour, nothing. But there is something I can't quite put my finger on.... And I can think of no-one else with more reason to kill Price."

Judd stared out the window at the Crown Court building.

"If Croswell's car had been there all weekend, and he did kill Price, then he must have got back here another way. There are trains from Swansea to Gloucester around the clock that stop at Port Talbot. Jen, get the footage from CCTV at Port Talbot and Gloucester from 1.00 Saturday afternoon until say 8.00, run it through the face recognition program—see if we can get a match for Croswell."

"Yes, Sir."

"And Jen. You know what you said about a 'secret investigation'? Keep it secret. And would you be able to go to the cottage near Port Talbot this weekend? Tell Mrs. Jones you want to look at the cottage. You are looking for anything at all that might allow Croswell to look like he was there when he wasn't. Talk to Mrs. J. Get as much detail as you can on what Croswell's movements were. It's in your own time, Jen. The Super can't know about it."

There wasn't much else Judd could do. During his visit to Maisemore on Saturday, he had a good look around for CCTV cameras that might shed some light on the theory that someone

74

other than Ogden might be responsible for Price's death. Apart from at the White Horse Inn carpark, there's really none.

Now, other cases were coming across his desk, and his limited resources were being stretched in all directions. Unless Jen could come up with something, the game was going to play out, and Ogden was going to get life.

Even still, Judd was keen to find out if Farmer had found anything that might change the outcome. "What did you find on the railway CCTV? Anything of interest?"

"No Luck. We've scanned 14 hours of footage from Swansea, Port Talbot, and Gloucester stations, Saturday afternoon 1.00 to Sunday Morning 7.00. No match for Croswell. We used 11 photos of Croswell for each scan. Nothing."

"What about Buses?"

"None running that route in those times."

"Well, that's that. Maybe I'm barking up the wrong tree. David was right. There were a lot of people angry about Price getting off the murder charge. Perhaps it was someone else local. Or maybe it was Ogden, and I'm the one chasing shadows."

Judd was feeling torn between his duty to find the truth and convict the right person for the crime and his empathy for David, whom he considered to be a friend. Subconsciously, he hoped they would not find any incriminating evidence on him.

"Shall I still go to Port Talbot this weekend?"

"I don't know, Jen. I'll leave it up to you. It's in your time, anyway."

"I'll see how I feel on Saturday."

****

The following Monday, Judd started early to get through the mountain of paperwork piling on his desk. Jennifer Farmer arrived at 7.50. "Got a minute, gov?"

"Sure. Did you go?"

"Yes. I went down yesterday. It's a bit of a drive, but nice place there."

"Definitely. What did you find?"

"That Mrs. J. is a unit! A dog doesn't fart in the street without her noticing. She was really helpful. Gave me a complete rundown of the time Croswell was there – she's got a memory like a steel trap!

She saw him at 1.50 Saturday afternoon on his porch and then about 6.15 Sunday morning as he returned from his beach walk. She didn't see him again on Sunday and saw him walking on the beach Monday morning. Apparently, he walks early every morning."

"What about in the cottage, anything there of interest?"

"Not a lot. But a couple of things I noticed. There is a bit of dust on everything. But the plugs on the lamps in the living room and bedroom were dusted like they had been unplugged and plugged back in. The cassette player on the stereo looks like it was used, no dust on the buttons. And the record player had been used, finger marks on the lid. I found that unusual."

"You would. I'm surprised someone your age even knows what cassettes and vinyl records are. Croswell told me he uses it to play his old music cassettes and vinyls. Not unusual for someone that lived through the 70s & 80s. I've still got a box of them myself."

"Really?"

"Really. You just can't beat the sound from a vinyl record. And Mrs. J heard him playing Pink Floyd on Saturday night, and I saw the record still on the turntable on Sunday morning."

"That doesn't mean he was necessarily there. He could have started it on a timer or something."

"Yes, but he still had to be there. Mrs. J was adamant that he played the whole album."

"So?"

"So, you can't play the whole album unless you are there to turn the record over to side two when side one finishes. Have you never played a vinyl record, Jen?"

"Err…. No. They actually have *two* sides?"

"They do. So, Croswell must have been there at around 10.pm." Judd was keen to move on. "Anything else?"

"There's a couple of bicycles in the storeroom at the back. Mrs. J says she keeps them there for her guests. Apparently, he went for a short ride Saturday morning to the shop to get a paper. She said he has always done that when he is there at the weekend – if the weather's ok. It's about a forty-minute ride – there and back. He got back at about 8.35."

"Yes, she told me that, too. Nothing unusual there."

"No, but it shows that he did have an alternative form of transport to his car. Although, when I asked Mrs. J about it, she said she would know if David went anywhere on the bike because she would see the tracks in the sand on the track."

"Yes, and I doubt he rode it all the way to Maisemore and back. I'll leave that outside the realms of possibility for now. Thanks, Jen. Take an early minute today."

"Thanks Gov. There's something else. I checked out the daughter, Judy's, alibi. I spoke to Janice Carruthers. Seems Judy was there for dinner on Saturday night, but she left shortly before 9.00, complaining of a headache. She said she would walk home as it was only a five-minute walk. Her husband, James stayed until around 10.30. That would have given her time to drive to Maisemore in time to kill Price at around 9.20."

"Hmmm …that is interesting."

"Shall we bring her in, Gov?"

"No. but talk to her neighbours. See if they heard her car leave or return around those times."

"Yes Gov."

****

Ogden was remanded in custody until his trial on July 27th. No information that could incriminate anyone for Price's murderer other than Ogden could be found, so he faced court with a huge body of evidence against him. Judd sat in the courtroom as proceedings unfolded, and the evidence against Ogden was described in detail. Judd was surprised to see David Croswell in the public area. He was listening intently to the evidence and feverishly scribbling notes. At the lunch adjournment, David was sitting on the bench in front of the court when Judd joined him. "I suppose I shouldn't be surprised to see you here, but what is with all the note-taking?"

"Research. For a really curly yarn I'm working on."

"A 'True Crime' story?"

"Not really. It will be fiction, but based on real events. You gave me the idea for it. You'll be first to get a free copy."

"I look forward to it. They're going back in now; I'll see you later."

"Sure, Mick."

79

The trail was extended to a second day, with Ogden's lawyer maintaining that Ogden did not send the messages to Price and that the other evidence was planted on him. But really, he had no proof to back it up. All the messages were sent from the areas that Ogden was known to be in at the time they were sent, and the fact that his phone was turned off much of the time was not unusual because many of the sites he worked on had a phone ban. Dr. Paul Morris, the linguist, said that he could not say for certain that Ogden hadn't written the messages. They were within the styles he had used previously.

Ogden had pleaded Not Guilty and maintained his innocence. But there was a stack of strong evidence linking him to the murder and only his word on anything that could prove his innocence. And given his history, his word didn't carry a lot of credibility.

At the end of the morning session, the court was adjourned, and the jury sent to consider their verdict. They returned barely an hour later. Ogden sat silently in the witness box, staring at the floor. He knew what was coming.

"We find the defendant Guilty as Charged." The foreman announced when asked by the Judge.

David Croswell watched as the handcuffed Ogden was led from the witness box. Ogden looked up directly at Croswell and mouthed some words to him that only two people in the room saw. *'You did this.'*

Croswell knew exactly what he said, and so did Judd.

Sentencing was scheduled for the following Thursday.

Outside the court, Croswell came up to Judd, who was about to cross the road to the police station. "Good Result?"

Judd looked straight ahead. "I just hope we got the right guy, Dave." He said with a look that said he still suspected Ogden had been set up. David watched him cross the intersection and disappear into the police building. He knew Judd still suspected him.

If only he knew what the truth was. David thought. And then, a most tantalising prospect entered his writer's mind. *What if I tell him what the truth is? In the guise of fiction, of course. That is a delicious idea.*

Ogden got 'life' with ten years non-parole period.

****

Part 5. Truth

Following Daniel Price's acquittal............

David watched as Daniel Price drove away in a car full of his cohorts. *If he thinks he's got away with murder, he is very mistaken!* He thought as he waited by the car where Judy was feeding baby David. After saying her goodbyes to husband James, she turned to her father. "Come on, dad. Let's go home. I'll drive."

They drove in silence to Maisemore and up Old Rd. to David's home. Judy made a pot of tea.

"What are you going to do now, dad?" she asked, pouring 2 cups.

"Carry on, I suppose. Unless the police can find any more evidence, there is nothing the law can do to give us some closure. How are you feeling about it, Jude?"

"Frustrated - Angry. I know Price is guilty. That's obvious. The only problem is, what's obvious isn't proof. Not for a court, anyway. There must be some way we can get justice for mum. I feel like killing him myself for what he's done."

"Careful, Jude. If I think of anything, I'll let you know."

Judy sat next to David and leaned on her father's shoulder. "I miss mum. She never got to see baby David. It's so cruel!" she said through tears that rolled down her cheeks and dripped onto her blouse.

"I know, darling. I miss her too. So much it hurts." The lump hardened in David's throat, and tears swelled up in his eyes. But his creative mind was working—forming a plan.

David and Judy talked through the afternoon, the main subject being getting some closure and justice for Marion.

As they talked, David's mind was creating a strategy, a scenario that would make both Price and Ogden pay. Being a crime fiction writer gave him many insights into the workings of the criminal mind - and the detective's. Any action he took would need to be absolutely watertight, not a trace to connect him with anything.

He had studied forensic science on-line in the final years of his teaching career in preparation for his writing past-time. His first book had not been a great success, but enough to get his name recognised. His second and third books sold well enough to provide a living income, and he was looking forward to a happy life with Marion for many years. Unfortunately, that part of his vision was cruelly snuffed out. And the ensuing legal process had all but extinguished his focus on the fourth book. Now, it had to go on hold until the fire of injustice inside him was quelled.

It was near dinner time when it was time for Judy to leave.

"I'd better get home, dad. James is on call after 7. And little David needs to relieve my discomfort. I'm near bursting. I'll get let-down on the way home at this rate."

"Thanks for staying with me this afternoon. It's been a kick in the guts."

"I know, Dad. Love you."

As Judy backed her silver BMW out of the drive, David was sad, but excited. A most devious plot was circulating in his mind.

The next morning, David drove to Gloucester and parked in the staff car park at King's. They still let him park there as an unofficial favour for his 34 years of service and he had lifetime access to the library. But instead of using the library Wi-Fi for internet as he often did, he walked a short distance to an internet café that had its own interfaces. There could be no tracing his searches. Having bought a coffee and paid for an hour of internet, he created a new Gmail account in the name of 'John Jory' and then typed in the search bar 'hyper-realistic masks'.

There is a myriad of sellers of these silicone masks, with a range of prices and qualities, some good suppliers in Amsterdam, but the best he could find were from an Italian supplier. On their enquiry form, he asked, *'Do you make custom-fitted masks?'*

The answer came to his new Gmail inbox within a few minutes, with the information that they could make masks custom-fitted to the user's face that can be made to look like any celebrity or person that they have detailed photos of. They would need the user to sit for a mould to be taken from their head and shoulders. The average cost is around €3200, depending on hair and features.

This price was more than he expected, but the mask had to be absolutely convincing. Also, he would need to pay in cash to keep the purchase untraceable; and would have to go to Milan for a fitting.

The first job was to get some cash. Marion's Mercedes was hardly ever used these days, and he had been thinking of selling it for some time. He only kept it for sentimental value. Now was the time to convert it to cash for a good sentimental reason. The next day, he washed and vacuumed it, took some nice photos, and listed it on the local trader for £9900—cash only. This was at least £1000 below any similar car on the market.

Not surprisingly, the next day, David received four enquiries, and the following day, he watched it drive away with £9800 cash in his hand.

In the morning, he went to his garage and pulled from the shelf a box of stuff that really should have been thrown out years ago. In it, he found two of his old iPhones. He plugged them in to charge, and proceeded to remove any files from their memory, embedded settings, and the SIM cards. When they were fully charged, he put them in his backpack. He left his usual phone at home on the charger and drove to Worcester. No one would recognise him up there. He stopped at a petrol station and used bought a £50 pre-paid SIM card with monthly roll-over credit for one of the phones.

"Cash or card?" the attendant asked.

"Cash"

He proceeded across town to a 24-hr store and bought a similar SIM card for the other phone. He was not required to provide any ID for either SIM card.

He then found an internet café. He opened google images and did a search for William Ogden. There was an amazing amount of people with that name. He would need a different approach. He knew Ogden could often be found at the White Horse Inn on a Friday or Saturday night, less so since his falling out with Price, though. David went to the pub the following Friday evening and was chatting with the publican, Barry, when Ogden walked in with one of his workmates.

"Here's your mate now." Barry quipped.

"Yeah, good one, Barry," David answered sarcastically and took his pint of lager to a table that had a good view of Ogden at the bar. While pretending to be writing a message on his phone, he took several dozen photos of Ogden, with as much detail as possible. He took note of Ogden's clothes. A blue flannelette shirt, a black duffle coat with the top left-hand button missing and a tear in the right-hand back flap.

Something else I need to check out while he's here at the pub. David thought. He took his empty glass to the bar.

"Cheers, Barry. I'll see you later, eh..."

"Cheers, Dave."

David noticed Ogden watching him as he left the pub. He drove home and then walked back down Old Road and across the road to Ogden's flat, proceeding to the narrow laneway that ran behind the row of units. He looked around in the twilight—no one in sight. Opening the rear gate, he noted that the latch was broken and couldn't be locked. He scanned the small yard. A small garden shed was in the back corner. Not much in it but a few tools, a bicycle, and an old kitchen sideboard-type cupboard. There was a mat on the back doorstep, a broom leaning against the wall and a pair of well-worn work boots near the door. A clothesline across the yard held three Hi-Viz shirts, some socks and underwear, and a jacket.

David left and walked home.

The next morning, he left his phone at home and went into Gloucester to the internet café, got a coffee, and opened his new Gmail account. He messaged the Italian mask supplier again:

'I can come in around two to four weeks' time for head and shoulder mould. I need two masks. One I will select from your stock faces, and the other will be of the person shown in the attached files. I will pay cash 50% on order and the remainder on completion if that is suitable to you. Please advise appointment time and date for sitting.'

****

A former classmate and cricket teammate of David's, George Archibald, was now living in Amsterdam and had often extended an invitation to him to visit. He and his wife Eve had come over for Marion's funeral, and they pleaded with David to come and stay for a week or so, and David agreed to take him up on the offer – one day. Now that day was approaching.

The next week, he had a firm appointment for his mould sitting in about four weeks. He called George.

"Hello George, how are things over there?"

"Just fine and dandy, thanks, Dave. So, when are you coming to see us?" George asked, expecting the same lame excuses from David that he had got for the past nine months.

"Well, funny you should ask, Geo. I was thinking of coming in three weeks."

"Three weeks! Really! You're not winding me up, are you?"

"Definitely not, mate. Do you still have that spare room available?"

"Of course! Come and stay as long as you like. Eve and I would love to have you here."

"Thanks, George, that's great. I'll be there on a Tuesday. Just a couple of things, though. I have to catch the train south for a few days, got a bit of research for my new book to do, and then I can be back for a week or so."

"That is just fabulous, Dave. Send me your flight details, and I'll pick you up from the airport, ok. The taxis are a shit-fight from hell - don't even think about it."

"Capital, Geo. Can't wait. Tell Eve I expect one of her legendary *King's Spring Fair award-winning tea cakes* on arrival." David joked.

"Done Job. You won't be disappointed. See you then. Bye Dave."

Judy invited David over for dinner on Friday night, which was always a great time to catch up with his adorable granddaughter and ogle at his baby grandson. Over dinner, David told them the news. "I'm going to visit George and Eve in Amsterdam for a couple of weeks. "They've been at me for months to come over. Might get a bit of time on the continent to do a bit of research for the new book. Will you be alright without my child-minding while I'm away?"

"Sure, Dad," Judy replied. "It will do you good to get away. Be sure to send George and Eve our love, and remember to show them lots of baby photos. When are you going?"

"I've got a 2.45 flight out of Bristol on Tuesday 28th. I'll catch the train down. Would you be able to bring me to the station, Jude?"

"No problem, just give me the time."

"How did you go selling the Merc?" James asked.

"Fabulous. £9800. Sold it in a day."

"Too cheap! Should have asked 12 grand."

"Yes, probably should have. But I'm kind of relieved to see it go. It had become an uncomfortable reminder, somehow. Can't really explain it."

"I get it, dad," Judy added. "'Moving on' stuff."

"Anyway, it will make a space in the garage for an over-priced, self-indulgent, highly impractical sports car." David quipped. "I'm liking the idea of a DB5."

"Well, your next book better be a good one," James said.

"It's a bestseller in waiting." David chuckled.

The next morning, David looked at himself in the mirror. He saw an overweight, middle-aged man looking back at him. He used to be so fit during his sporting days. Judy had been frequently reminding him of this fact; but getting fit never seemed important enough. Now something was making it very important. If he were to impersonate William Ogden, he needed to lose weight, fast. 25 pounds at least. Judy and James did karate lessons at a local studio. *"Why don't you come and check it out, at least"* Judy had often asked. He would join up today. Morning walks would become runs. Food and beer intake would need to reduce. This was important. David knew what it took to get fit and lose weight. *I've done it before; I can do it again. 25 pounds in 4 weeks? Not easy, but possible - with the right effort. I'll start tomorrow.*

****

David waited at the kerb of the pick-up rank at Amsterdam Airport. Shortly, a black Tesla pulled up beside him, and the passenger window slid down. "Hallo, welkom in nederland," George said is his best Dutch. The boot opened, David put his bag in, and the boot closed.

"Well done, Geo." David settled into the plush leather seat. "The job's going well then?" He perused the car's interior.

"Can't complain. They pay me an obscene amount of money for my expertise. Eve's at yoga, so we'll have an hour to ourselves before she gets home." George turned the near-silent car onto the N201 motorway towards Zandvoort.

Shortly they arrived at the beachside suburb, and George pulled into the drive of a modern two-storey home.

"Nice spot."

"Not too bad today, for March. It gets pretty damn miserable through the winter. It's a fantastic place if you're into howling arctic wind. Summer is great, though - for a few days. Eve's choice, of course, I'd be happy in the city."

The upstairs living room was fitted with modern leather furniture, an extensive bar, and shag-pile carpet reminiscent of the 1970s.

George got David a drink, "Still susceptible to a Glenfiddich, I assume?"

"Oh Yes."

"Nice view of the sea from up here," David said as he sipped his scotch, standing at the window.

"Good on the odd days when you can actually see it!" George added. "Now, tell me, old chap, how are things, you know, since...... since you are on your own."

"I have my days. Some days are diamonds, some days are stone."

"John Denver." George chuckled. "I've still got the album. Any advancements on the culprit?"

"It's a cold case now. I don't think the police are pursuing anything. Even though we are all pretty sure who did it, that's the thing about the law and the justice system. Knowing in your heart what the truth is, doesn't constitute proof. They need absolute proof. I guess there have been many cases where, even with what looks like proof, innocent people have been convicted of crimes they didn't commit. In fact, that's the theme of my new book."

"Interesting, how does the story go?"

"Ahh, you'll have to wait until it's finished. Even I don't know yet. But I'll just say that it explores the contradiction of moral justice and legal justice."

"It should be a winner. You said you had to go south for a few days."

"Yes, I'll catch the train to Paris on Saturday. Some of my story is set there, and I want to check out some details. Some readers are always looking for ways to trip me up. I should be back on Thursday. I'll let you know."

"No problem, Dave. In the meantime, you've got the run of the house. I do all my work from home now, so if you want to use the car, it's there for you."

"Thanks, but you drive on the wrong side of the road, so I'll probably give that a miss. I'll be doing a bit of writing while I'm here, anyway."

"Well, you write while I work, and the rest of the time, we can have a jolly good time."

"Sounds good to me." David relaxed into a recliner chair. "That aroma…. is that what I think it is?"

"We promised you an award-winning tea cake. Yes, that's it baking."

The two men chatted until Eve arrived home, still a little flushed from her yoga workout. She was looking fit and healthy and about 20 years younger than her years.

"Dave! Lovely to see you at last! Wow! You're looking in good nick. What have you been doing?"

"Good food and exercise. I walk every morning, been doing karate, would you believe? Judy has just about converted me into a Vegan – vegetarian, at least. And what about you? You look younger than when I saw you last."

"You always know the right thing to say to a woman," George interjected, "Have you two finished your mutual-admiration session?"

"Just getting warmed up." Eve teased. "Are you hungry?"

"I feel tea and cake coming on," David said. "Yes, please."

****

On Saturday morning, George dropped David at the railway station. "Thanks, George. I'll see you Thursday if nothing changes."

He bought a return ticket to Paris with his credit card.

On the journey to Paris, he dozed, the components of his plan gaining clarity in his mind. There were risks, but he knew how to mitigate them. Create diversions, false trails that go nowhere.

David walked the 2.5 km from Gare de Nord to the Hotel. A short walk by his norm, and welcome activity after sitting for 3 hours. He carried only a backpack with his laptop, toiletries, and a couple of changes of clothes.

At the desk, the clerk asked. "aurez-vous besoin d'un petit-déjeuner?"

"Yes, thank you. Breakfast each of the five days." David observed the blank look on the clerk's face.

"Oui merci. petit-déjeuner chacun des cinq jours"

"Oui monsier. Chambre 341. Bonne journée."

Do they not know any English or just pretend that they don't to piss us off? David thought as he waited for the lift. *If I can learn their language, why can't they learn ours?*

After breakfast the next morning, he emailed the mask supplier again to check that his appointment the following day was still valid. All was well. In the afternoon, David left the hotel, leaving his mobile phone on the charger in his room and the "do not disturb" tag on his door. He took the underground to Gare de Leon and used cash to buy a ticket for a premium sleeper cabin on the night train to Milan. It left Paris at 7.15 pm and arrived in Milan at 6.00 am. His appointment was for 10 am and would take about two hours. That should give him plenty of time to catch the 14.40 train that will have him back in Paris by 10 pm.

It was 5.30 pm. A bit under two hours before he left for Milan. His body belt wallet was stuffed with 7000 Euros. He walked to a café near the Notre Dame and bought a meal with his card.

The whole trip went exactly as plan. The sleeper was comfortable and secure, and David slept well. He found his way to the studio in plenty of time and had the head and shoulders cast made. He selected a face from their stock masks and made sure that the photos of Ogden were satisfactory for that mask. All was in order.

Not wanting to make another trip or send cash by post, David decided to pay the whole amount in cash on the day. €1400 for the stock face and €3300 for the Ogden mask. Less than he had expected, not realising that the stock face would be much cheaper. It was a leap of faith, but this studio was a highly reputable organisation, supplying to theatre companies the world over. He arranged to have the masks sent to George and Eve's address in Amsterdam.

"There is one thing I must insist on." He said before handing over the cash. After you have made my masks, you destroy the mould you make of my head."

"We always do." The man replied. We digitise the exact shape, though, for future reference."

"Then you must promise me that you not only destroy the mould, but do not keep a digital record, or a record of the man's face I have supplied photos of either. This is purely for privacy reasons. I ask that you respect my wishes in this regard."

"Certainly, Mr. Jory. Although that is the opposite to what most of our customers request."

"I understand, but I have promises to keep. When you have made my masks, please confirm that no digital or other records of my purchase have been kept."

"Yes, Mr. Jory. We will do that for you."

David watched as they counted out the cash.

"All correct, sir."

"Thank you, Goodbye."

When the train pulled into Gare de Lyon at 10.02 that evening, David was feeling tired but excited. The major investment in his plan was made. Now he had to overcome all apprehensions and follow through. It was for Marion. And Judy. And it was the only way he could see to quell the fire of injustice burning inside him. A taxi took him back to the Hotel. David was tired – but hungry too – and keen to make a traceable purchase. A nearby restaurant was the answer to both.

The next few days were spent lazily sightseeing and hanging out in Paris, soaking up the local culture and atmosphere. The French lifestyle looks so similar to the English in many ways, but there is something about the French people that the Brits lack. They seem much prouder of their Frenchness than Brits are of their Britishness. They seem to make more time for each other—value social interaction more. They see 'Having a coffee' for 2 hours as a valuable use of their time.

All the while, he was planning the next steps. It all had to come together perfectly. He searched a few second-hand clothing stores until he found what he was looking for a black duffle coat the same as Ogden's. He studied the photos of Ogden and modified the coat to look exactly like his.

The next week in Amsterdam was a delightful time with his good friends, and he wondered why he hadn't taken up their offer earlier. But it ended all too soon – as holidays always do. George drove David to the airport on a chilly Wednesday morning.

"There's a package addressed to John Jory coming to your address," David advised. "Can you put it in a post bag and send it on to me, George?"

"Sure, no problem. John Jory??"

"Hah! It's a pen name I was going to use once. I still use it for some internet purchases – it matches an eBay username. It's just some stuff I ordered online. I thought it would get here before I left. I didn't send it home in case it got there before I got back."

"Easy. Consider it done."

****

David went to his garage and opened the box he had sarcastically labelled "Stuff I should have thrown out" to appease Marion and found an old leather wallet. He folded up a number of sheets of printer paper and stuffed them in the wallet until it bulged healthily. He wrote a note on a small piece of paper and wrapped it around a £10 note. He drove to Gloucester and caught the train to Birmingham.

In Birmingham, he put the wallet in his back pocket. The top of the wallet was just above the pocket seam. David walked around, went to supermarkets and parks, ate at the food hall, had tea and cake at cafes, and stood on the bridge overlooking the canal. He had just walked a bustling street near the railway station when he noticed that the wallet was gone.

A young lad had been watching him for a while. He had seen the bulging wallet and followed David around for about an hour – waiting for the right moment. In the busy street, he made his move. Bumping into David slightly as he passed, it was enough of a distraction to slip the wallet out of his pocket without him noticing. He pocketed the wallet and nonchalantly walked away.

David sat on a bench in the park and waited. Fifteen minutes later, he got the call he was after. 'No Caller ID' He answered the old iPhone.

"What the fuck is this, a set-up? 10 pounds?! And a heap of paper?"

"Calm down. Obviously, you read the note."

"Yes."

"Well, are you interested in making £500 for one small pocket-picking?"

"Yes, but not if it's a set-up to get me arrested."

"It's not. I suppose you'll just have to trust me on that. Well….are you interested, or not? I'm quite happy to find another pickpocket and give them the £500. But you picked me, clean as a whistle. I genuinely didn't notice it going. You are good at your craft."

"I'll take that as a compliment. What would I have to do?"

"You would need to catch the train to Gloucester on a Wednesday evening. Go to a specific pub and find a specific man. He always carries his phone in his back pocket, and he's always at the same pub Wednesday nights - payday. I need you to pick his phone, take it to a locker in the railway station – I'll give you the code. You put the phone in the locker, take the envelope with the money and catch the train home. You are going to have to trust me that the money will be there. I'm going to have to trust you that you get the phone first and don't rip me off. You can definitely trust me on one thing – if you rip me off, you're going down – hard. I'm well connected. I had someone follow me and video you before you picked me. We can find you. Believe me. It wouldn't be worth £500 to cross me. Your side of the deal is secure – if the money's not there, you don't leave the phone."

"That sounds like a fair deal. I'm in."

"You know how to avoid showing your face to CCTV, I assume?"

"Give me a break!"

"Ok. Silly question. Here's another one. Can you crack the passcode on an iPhone?"

"In less than 60 seconds."

"Great. I need you to leave the passcode and let me know what it is, then turn it off before you leave the pub."

"All good. When do you want this job done?"

"In about four- or five-weeks' time. I'll let you know. I want to avoid any trace of you to this job, so I'll give you a phone to use. You are not to use it for any other purpose than communication with me, do you understand? Nothing whatsoever. When you drop the picked phone, you drop this one as well, ok? You don't know me. I don't know you. We've never met. There will be no trace to connect us. The phone is in locker 456 at Birmingham central. The locker code is 9999, same as phone passcode. The charger cable is there too. Pick it up anytime in the next week. Keep it with you. Check it often. I don't know when I will contact you. There is only one number in the contacts, this one. Are we all good?"

"Yes, I think so."

"Spiffing. I'll send you all details as required in a couple of weeks. And, for fuck's sake, do not mention this job to anyone, ok? Not your mates, not your bird, no-one. Your future health is tied to your silence, get it?"

"Loud and clear."

"Good. I'll be in touch."

****

David's son-in-law, James, has a sister, Shirley, whose husband, Peter, owns a removal and courier business. The last family Christmas lunch was at their home in Cheltenham. Peter mentioned that he was renewing his fleet and had a number of smaller vans that he used very little. David gave him a call.

"Hello Peter, it's David. David Croswell. How are you?"

"Good Thanks, Dave. How can I help you?"

"Well, you know, at Christmas, you were saying that you had some vans that you didn't use much. I was wondering if I could borrow one for a few days in a couple of weeks' time. I got a bit of stuff to move around."

"Sure, Dave. That's not a problem. Actually, I've got 2 Hi-Aces that we're about to strip the signage off to get them ready to sell. You could borrow one of those. Just let me know when you want it."

"Thanks a lot, Pete. That will save me a shirt-load of stuffing around."

"Any time, Dave. Bye."

****

The pieces of the plan were falling into place. On April 20th, a package arrived from Amsterdam. This is what he was waiting for. Dave carefully opened the inner package and removed the latex masks. He couldn't wait to try them on.

He stood in front of the mirror and pulled the stock face mask over his head. It fitted exactly to his face and shoulders. It was like a second skin. The masks themselves were surprisingly thin and flexible.

He talked. The mask talked. He smiled. The mask smiled.

"I'm going to call you 'John'." He said with a chuckle. "You can be John Jory."

It was so life-like he had to remove it to make sure it was still him underneath. Then he fitted the Ogden mask.

"Fucking Hell!" he said out loud, looking in the mirror. "Jesus! I've become him. I'm William Ogden."

He moved his mouth and eyes. He had to remind himself that this was a mask. Everything looked just like a real face right down to the short beard stubble, the scar under the left eye, the oily, unkempt hair.

The latex mask was porous, and the makers claim it will even let sweat through it. They guarantee that it will pass face recognition scans. David could see why. He carefully removed it and put it back in its cotton bag. Then he stowed both in a box in the garage cupboard.

He had to set a date for the completion of the plan. The way it was panning out, it looked like the weekend of 13th, and 14th May was going to work. Coincidentally, this was the date exactly one year from when Marion was murdered.

How incredibly perfect! David mused.

For some years, David and Marion had used a seaside cottage near Port Talbot for a weekend getaway or a summer break. Although not high class by any measure, it was a beautiful, secluded place where the forces of nature were at your doorstep and in your nostrils. The fickle Atlantic Ocean has the power and presence to take you where she wants. To serene, tranquil balmy paradise, or terrifying vitriolic fury. All in all, a great place to write stories. He called the owner - Mrs. Jones - and booked the cottage for Friday 12th May until the following Tuesday.

There were just a few more ducks to get in a row.

Firstly, if he was to wear Ogden's boots, he had to make sure none of his DNA could be transferred to them. David went to the supermarket and bought two identical pairs of thin black socks and a box of skin-tone biodegradable surgical gloves—100 pack. He bought a large tube of silicone sealer at the hardware store and a pack of jumbo zip ties.

That night at home, David smeared his feet with a barrier cream and pulled on one of the pairs of socks. He squeezed a large amount of silicone sealer into his gloved hands and smeared it to completely cover the socks. Then, with fresh gloves, he pulled the second pair of socks over the others. Reclining in the chair, he watched a movie until the silicone had set.

The next day, David took a long-bladed carving knife from the kitchen and clamped it in his workshop vice, blunt side up. With a fine file, he filed the back of the knife to give it an edge on both sides. Then, using a knife sharpener, sharpened both edges to near razor sharpness. He wrapped it in a small towel and stashed it in the garage shelves.

****

He messaged the phone he had left with the unknown pickpocket. 'Can you do the job on Wednesday 10th May?'

A couple of hours later, the answer came back. 'Yes, what are the deets?'

David messaged back:

'He will be at the Dick Whittington on Westgate Street from about 5.00. He usually leaves about 9.00, sometimes earlier, sometimes later. It gets fairly busy after 6.00, so there will be lots of cover. Attached are photos of him. I'll send more photos and instructions a little later.'

David loaded more photos of Ogden and sent them with a message:

'There are 3 CCTV cameras in the pub. It might pay to do a reconnaissance visit to familiarise yourself with the layout. As soon as you get the phone, crack the passcode, and turn it off. Take it to the railway station, open a locker – I'll let you know which one on the day - with the code 9999. Leave the phone and the phone I gave you. Your payment is in the envelope in the locker. Close the locker and secure it with the same code, 9999. Catch the next train back to Birmingham. Do not hang around Gloucester splurging cash. I don't want any attention drawn to you, ok?'

The answer came immediately back:

'All clear'.

****

David called Peter. "Hello Pete, It's Dave. I've teed up to do this bit of moving stuff on the weekend of the 13th. Can I come and pick up that van on the Thursday before? I'll catch the train over in the morning if that's ok."

"All good, Dave. Just come to the front office. I should be there. If not, I'll leave the keys with Liz at the desk."

"Thanks, Pete. I owe you one. I should have it back on Monday. All going well."

"Whenever, Dave. We're not sending them to the auction house until next month, anyway. Buy me a beer one day if that will help you feel better."

"Cheers, Pete."

****

Now all the ducks were lined up. There was no backing out now. He had to follow through. For Marion. For Judy. For the grandchildren that would never know their grandmother. It felt strange. The planning was done and acted upon to get things ready. That was the easy bit.

David had a lingering doubt that he could do this. If he didn't, he would live a life of regret with the pain of injustice burning inside him. That was sure to make him sick. If he did it and got found out, would it be worth it? He pondered this quandary. Yes. Even if he got found out, it would still be worth it. The days seem to pass painfully slowly until it was time to act, then it seemed the day had come too soon. One thing only was clear—this had to be done.

David awoke at 6.00 am on Wednesday 10th May. He dressed in his exercise gear as he did every morning, and jogged his usual route, up Old Road, into Church Road, around the back of the Business Centre to The Rudge, back to the main road at the White Horse Inn, and up the A417 back to Old Road.

He made some breakfast and tea. Then he messaged his pickpocket: 'All good for tonight?'

Shortly, the answer came: 'All set'.

David was uncomfortable in trusting a known criminal, but he had no choice now. It was a waiting game.

He anxiously waited out the day, and at 9.00 pm, he fitted the 'John' mask and put on a black hoodie. He left his phone at home, took the old prepaid phone with him, and drove to Gloucester station. On the way, he received a message:

'Done. passcode is 1234'

He parked two streets away from the station. It was 9.35 when he ventured in – the hood pulled over his head to hide the face from CCTV cameras. He went to the locker area and to locker 112. Would it be there? Dare he check, for fear that it wasn't?

David nervously entered the code - 9999. The locker opened. There inside were two phones. Relief. He pocketed them both and walked from the station, head down, hood obscuring the face.

The next morning, David packed a small backpack with a thermos of tea, a ham and cheese sandwich, and the bag containing the 'John' mask. In a sports bag he packed the zip ties, gloves, a large pair of scissors, the duffle coat and a few other items. He caught the train to Cheltenham, arriving just after 8.am. As it turned out, Peter was not in the office, but Liz was expecting him and had the keys.

"Out the back of the yard, the plate number is on the key tag."

"Thanks, Liz. Let Pete know I've picked it up."

Dave drove out of town towards Swansea. Storm clouds rose into a blue sky in the distance. *Storm brewing.* He thought. *Not just the weather.* He pulled onto a side road near Clydach and stopped for a cup of tea and a snack. Before setting off again, he put on 'John'.

It was raining heavily before Swansea, with wipers slapping a rhythmic beat, he turned towards Port Talbot and parked the van in the carpark of the Neath Port Talbot Hospital. Rain squalls came and went as he waited in the van for the weather to let up. It was only a 5-minute walk to the railway station, but he didn't want to get saturated on the way. Eventually, he had to seize the moment, and with the collar pulled up against the wind, he locked the van and walked quickly to the railway station, just dodging the next squall. The train back to Gloucester left in 3 minutes. Driving back home from Gloucester, he pulled over and removed 'John'. The mask was getting very uncomfortable after 4 hours in it. It was after 4.30 when he arrived home.

That evening, he walked to a spot not far from Ogden's home and turned on his phone wearing surgical gloves. He looked back through various messages sent to get a good idea of his language, abbreviation habits, etc., and checked whether Daniel Price's number was in his contacts. Luckily, it was. He turned the phone off and returned home.

Later, in the twilight, he returned to the same place and sent a message to Daniel Price. *This had better work.* He thought.

David was acutely aware that it may not, and the whole game would be off – or postponed, at least.

He took Ogden's phone with him on his morning walk at 6 am. When he passed near Ogden's home, he turned it on briefly to see that Price had replied. *Great. I'll message him back in a while.* He turned it off again.

After breakfast, he left his phone at home and took Ogden's with him to Gloucester, parking across the road from the construction site that he knew Ogden was working at. He briefly turned on his phone with surgical gloves on, sent another message to Price, turned it off, and drove home.

David packed his bags for his stay at Port Talbot, clothes, a laptop, some music cassettes, and vinyl albums, and an old cassette he used years ago to record his ideas. He went to the garage, found a box of electrical things, and fished out four old mechanical-type timer switches. He loaded everything in his car, including the box containing the masks. Just after midday, he headed down the A40 towards Swansea. He checked the fuel gauge—¼ full. *I'd better get some on the way.* He thought.

At the supermarket in Swansea, David bought food and beverage supplies for the week, then headed out through Port Talbot, checking the hospital carpark as he passed to make sure that the borrowed van was still there. He arrived at Mrs. J's farmhouse a little before 4.30.

"Welcome back, David. It's been a while. Did you have a good trip?"

"Yes, thanks. How have you been, Mrs. J? I haven't seen you for a year."

"I get by. My son comes over to help with maintenance. I was so sorry to hear about Marion. I sent flowers – for the funeral. I wish I had got to know her better those times she was here."

"Thank You, Mrs J, it was much appreciated. And, if there's anything I can do while I'm here, let me know. Have you got anyone else in next week? I may want to stay a few extra days."

"No. not yet. I'll tell you if anything comes in."

"I want to get a lot of writing done this weekend. I'd appreciate no interruptions. Thanks, Mrs. J."

"I absolutely understand. Do you have everything you need? I'll be going into town tomorrow."

"I think so. I went to the supermarket on the way. If I need anything, you'll be the first to know."

David settled into the cottage and went for an evening walk on the beach. Something about the smell of the ocean, the relentless sound of waves crashing on the shore, the constant screeching of seabirds, the brisk breeze in his hair created clarity and purpose combined with a powerful feeling of calm. The sun had set before he got back to the cottage. He made some dinner and sat on the sofa, planning the next day. The time had come. Time to even the ledger. Time to release the anguish of knowing Marion's killer walked free, and the man who prevented his prosecution to pay for his lies. He felt like he had a dirty stain on his life that he was about to wash clean. Hours passed.

Suddenly David realised it was after 10 pm and he would need to get a good night's rest for the next day. Strangely, he slept soundly and peacefully, in stark contrast to the storm that the following day would bring.

At 5.59 am, he awoke in time to turn his alarm off before it sounded at 6.00. He dressed and headed out for his morning walk on the beach. The sun peeked through the clouds on the horizon behind the hills. David walked, but soon broke into a jog and then into a full-tilt run. He ran a half-mile or so to the rocks at the southern end of the beach, where he stopped to catch his breath. He felt so good today – energised – empowered.

Returning to the cottage, he expected to see Mrs. J out walking as she normally does, but not this morning. He had breakfast and went to the storeroom at the back and retrieved a bicycle, checked the tyres, and walked it along the sandy track to the gate where the sealed road started. Fifteen minutes later, he was in the town with a coffee and a weekend paper. He stowed the paper in his backpack and rode back to the cottage—time to get to work.

David installed the mechanical timers to the power outlets feeding the standard lamps in the living room and desk lamp in the bedroom, setting the living room lamps to go off at 10.47 pm and the bedroom lamp to come on for 5 minutes from 10.45. He installed another timer on the supply to the stereo unit, put a cassette in the player, and pressed down the 'play' button. He set the time for 9.25 pm.

After testing that everything was working properly, he packed a backpack with the things he would need: the modified knife that he wrapped in a handtowel, both masks, a shirt, a pair of jeans, the sealed socks, and a woollen jumper. Everything else he needed was already in the van: A black duffle coat, biodegradable surgical gloves, boot covers, scissors, jumbo zip ties, paper bags, and garbage bags. He made a cup of tea and sat at the table on the front verandah, reading the paper. Mrs. Jones would be along shortly on her way into town.

When she came passed the cottage, she stopped and wound down the passenger side window. "I see you've been into town already," she called, indicating the bicycle tracks in the sand.

"Yes. I got my paper. Off to lunch with the widows club?"

"Yes, as usual. I'm doing some shopping after lunch – do you need anything?"

"No thanks, Mrs. J. I'm all good. I'm going to have a rest this afternoon. I didn't sleep well last night."

"Very well. I'll be quiet when I get back, then." Mrs. J drove off down the road.

David waited 15 minutes, then donned the backpack and collected the bicycle. He carried the bike to the gate, walking on the grass at the side of the track, so as to not leave any evidence of his departing. He rode to the hospital carpark, put the bicycle in the back of the van, and drove off down the M4 towards Cardiff.

In Cardiff, David drove around to determine the location of two places: A 24 hr laundrette and a Salvation Army donation bin. He had all afternoon to prepare, so he got some lunch and hung out by the pier. At 4 pm, he headed for Gloucestershire.

A few miles out from Maisemore, he pulled over into a side road and pulled on the 'John' mask. In Maisemore, he stopped on the A417 near Ogden's home, turned on his phone, and sent a message to Price. This was the turning point.

He waited anxiously, hoping no-one would walk by, curious as to who was parked there—especially Ogden. The phone beeped. It was the answer he was looking for. Now, he had to find somewhere to wait. His home was just around the corner, but he couldn't risk going there. Gloucestershire Royal Hospital carpark was the best bet. People waiting in cars was a common thing there. No one would notice.

David parked at the extreme edge of the carpark, laid the seat back, and had a rest. Nothing to do for two hours or so. Big night ahead. Two hours of sleep would be very useful. The mask was uncomfortable, but he could not risk being identified. Most of

Gloucester would recognise him by sight. He rested, but didn't sleep, the planned events ahead ever circulating in his mind.

Shortly after 8.30, David drove to Maisemore and parked the van off the road behind the church. It was beginning to get dark and black clouds filled the western sky. *If I'm lucky, we will get some rain later.*

He knew that the football was on the TV and Ogden would be watching it. This was the most dangerous part of the plan. He removed the 'John' mask and fitted the Ogden mask, put on the chequered shirt and duffle coat, and a pair of clear surgical gloves. He was William Ogden to anyone who saw him. Then David walked the length of Church Road across the A417 and to the alley behind Ogden's house. He removed his boots in the alley and went inside the yard to the back door, where he exchanged his boots for Ogden's. He could hear the sound of the football game finishing on the TV coming from inside the flat.

In the alley, he put on Ogden's boots and switched Ogden's phone on. He made his way up Old Road to the track along the lake. For a year, he had not been able to face walking along the path where Marion died, but tonight was different—he had a job to do. A job that the criminal justice system could not do for him. This was for Marion.

As he approached the bench that overlooked the lake, he could see Price sitting there. He made a noise by scuffing the ground to get his attention. Price stood up.

"Ah, Billy. This is neat. Back here again a year later!"

David did the best impersonation of Ogden's voice he could muster. "Aye, Danny, it is."

Price reached out to shake his hand. "Friends?"

David knew he had a glove on his hand, and Price would notice, so he seized the moment. It was a move he had rehearsed a hundred times or more. Practiced over and over until he could do it without thinking.

He swung his leg around and kicked Price in the Solar Plexus in one swift karate trained move. Price fell to the ground in agony, struggling to breathe. David quickly jumped on him, rolling him face down, and pulled his hands behind his back and secured them with a zip tie. Price was trying to move, roll over. "What the fuck, Bill!" he tried to shout, but only managed a muffled mumble. David swiftly turned around and, sitting on his back, tied his feet together with another zip tie. David stood up and watched Price squirm his way onto his side, looking up at his attacker. "Fuck, Billy! What is this all about?!" Price retorted, finding his voice a little more.

David reached inside his shirt and grabbed the edge of the mask. He carefully pulled off the mask so that Price could see who he was. Price went a ghostly white as he realised who he was dealing with.

"Croswell!! What the Fuck?!"

"The 'stupid cow' has sent me on a mission." David said calmly, "You thought you had got away with murder. Let me assure you that you are mistaken. "You see, Daniel, you fucked with the wrong man. That 'Stupid Cow' was my beloved wife of 34 years. We went to school together. She was a beautiful, intelligent, loving woman. You took her from me, and now you will pay the ultimate price. You'll pay the price, Price.... get it? No, you probably don't."

David removed the knife from his pocket. Price's eyes followed it as he moved it to his ribcage.

"You should have told the truth, Dan," David said as he pressed the blade harder into Price's ribs. "You see, if you had confessed to what you did, you may have got ten, maybe only eight years in prison, but now, you may not have any more years anywhere."

"I didn't mean to kill her!" Price shouted. "I just thought she was knocked out. Please, I can't die yet."

"Why did you hit her at all, you fuckwit? Why didn't you just fucking leave her alone?"

"I don't know. I was pissed. I can't really remember."

"You are a snivelling low-life piece of shit. You lied to the police, you lied in court, you got your mate Ogden to lie for you, and then you smugly said, 'It's not every day you get away with murder'. Well, matey, guess what? You didn't get away with it."

117

David reached into Price's pocket and pulled out his phone. "What's your passcode, Dan?" David asked, pushing the point of the knife harder into his chest.

"Why the fuck should I tell you?!!" Price shouted.

"To give yourself a few more minutes of life." David calmly replied.

"4-5-7-9"

"Thank you." David opened the phone and the camera app. "Now, what is going to happen now, Dan, is you are going to record a video in which you confess to killing Marion Croswell. If you do it good, you may live to see the light of another day. If not, you've seen your last daylight already. Here you go, sit up and lean against the bench here, nice and comfy. Are you ready? Make it good. Tell them who you are and what you did here a year ago. Rolling!"

David hit the record button and got Price's face in the frame.

"Hello, I am Daniel Price. A year ago, when I was walking home from the pub with Billy Ogden, we came across a woman, Marion Croswell, walking by the lake here. I was pissed, and I hit her on the head with a tree branch and knocked her out. I took the cash from her purse and left. I didn't mean to kill her, just knock her out, that's all."

"Great, that will do nicely."

David pushed Price to the ground with his foot and rolled him onto his back. He waved the knife in front of his face and then carefully selected the right spot on his chest, right outside his heart.

"What are you doing?!! I thought you said I could live if I confessed."

'Sorry, I lied. Just like you did." David pressed the point of the knife into Price's chest. Price squirmed and tried to move.

"No! No! No! No!" Price shouted. "Please, No!"

"It's a bit late now. Perhaps you should have made some better choices when you had the chance, instead of being a smug arse-hole."

"They had nothin' on me. They couldn't prove I did it."

"No, but you did, didn't you? You fucked up big time, Daniel."

"Please!! Don't kill me. You've got my confession. I'll do the time!" Daniel's eyes went white with fear. His bladder released its contents.

"Like I said, all a bit late, now." The moment had arrived, and David hesitated. His greatest fear was always that when the moment arrived, he wouldn't be able to finish it. Fear set it. A hundred reasons not to kill Price flashed through his mind in an instant. *Had he covered everything? What would Judy think of him if she found out he was a murderer? Could he do the jail time if he got found out? Could he even kill him?* Price sensed his doubts

119

and seized the opportunity—a last-ditch chance to get out of this alive. "Ha. You are piss-weak, Croswell. You don't have the bottle."

That did it - David's eyes widened, and the blade plunged between Price's ribs, straight into his heart. Price let out a muffled yell, and his body spasmed, looking up at David briefly before rolling onto his face, driving the knife even further into his chest.

David rolled him onto his back with his boot. "That's from Marion." He said as the last signs of life faded from Price's face. His own heart was thumping, adrenalin coursing through his body. Sweat started to run down his chest. Panic set in. He'd just killed a man. Taken a life. No matter that it was justified. The law didn't see it that way. As much as this moment was rehearsed in his mind, the act of taking a life was still deeply disturbing. Darkness was closing in under heavy clouds. Momentarily the moon found a gap in the clouds and illuminated Price's dead face. *Must get away. Just a few small details to attend to.* What sounded like a snapping twig filled David's ears. Was someone coming? *Move! Now!* He turned off Price's phone and put it in a plastic bag, and stuffed it in his coat pocket.

He withdrew the knife from the lifeless body. There was a sucking noise as air was drawn into the chest cavity. David wrapped it carefully in a plastic bag he had brought for the purpose and stashed it in the duffle coat pocket. He rolled Price's body over twice with his boots until it was halfway down the bank of the lake.

He listened intently—only an owl hooting. *No footsteps. No time to waste.* He quickly put the Ogden mask back on and hurried along the path to The Rudge where Price's old blue van was parked, walked past houses where families watched television. Their life was normal, peaceful, uncomplicated. He had just killed a man. It felt like he was in a movie, but watching it at the same time. The world went black and white like in those infomercials when the bad product is shown. Inside the mask was a different world. David Croswell on the inside, William Ogden on the outside. It was weird. Apart from near the streetlights, there was darkness. A cold drizzle began to fall. David pulled his hood forward to keep the rain from his face, then realising he couldn't feel it anyway. The sweaty mask was becoming unbearable. *Quick. Get moving Dave.* He said to himself. *Get this done and be gone.*

At the end of the road was the White Horse Inn. Just before he got there, a woman walking turned into The Rudge and walked towards him. *Who is that? Would it be someone he knew? Or worse, someone that knew Ogden?* "Good evening," he said before realising that that was not something Ogden was likely to say, especially on his way home from killing someone. He was getting anxious, heart racing, sweating. The far -off sound of a siren near Gloucester filled his ears. *Fuck! Had someone found Price already and called the Police? It was possible. Got to get this job done. Now!*

As he cut across the carpark, he glanced up at the security camera, and continued up the road to Ogden's flat. The living room light was still on. In the alley, he removed Ogden's boots and carefully entered the backyard. He opened the door to the shed and slid the knife and Price's phone under the old timber cabinet. He crept to the back door and replaced Ogden's boots. Before picking up his own boots, he removed the gloves and stuffed them in his pocket. He pulled a fresh pair of gloves from the other pocket and pulled them on. He was always listening for any signs of movement from inside, but all he could hear was the TV. Some unknown movie was playing between commercial breaks.

David picked up his boots and carried them around to the front of the flat, making sure that no one was around. The siren had stopped. *Did that mean the police were still coming without their siren or that they weren't coming? It doesn't matter. Got to get out of here.* A man was walking along the road. David waited in the shadows until he was out of sight. Through the living room window, he could see Ogden, fast asleep on the sofa. A bong was on the table, along with several empty beer bottles. *Perfect.* David went to the front door and pushed Ogden's phone through the mail flap, willing it to land silently. It clunked loudly on the floor, but Ogden didn't stir. He removed his gloves again and put his boots on.

Now, to get out of here. David thought as he hastily made his way up Church Road towards the church, staying in the shadows wherever possible. The picture of Price's dead face flashed in his mind as he walked.

Headlights from an approaching car illuminated the trees that lined the road. *"Fuck!"* David dived into a small gap between the bushes just before the headlights came into view.

Got to get out of here. Sprinting up the road towards the church, he heard the sound of another car turning off the highway into Church Road. *Was this the police car? Jesus Christ! Nowhere to hide at this end of the road. Run. Run. Run!* He could see the church gates. The car was going into the dip in the road. When it came up the other side, the driver could see all the way to the churchyard. He'd be right in their headlights. *Five seconds, max. I won't make it if I go through the turnstile. Over the fence – only option.* Running straight at the stone fence, he dove over it as he heard the scrape of the car in the bump at the bottom of the dip. *Did they see me?*

The car screeched around the corner in front of the church and disappeared up the road. It wasn't the police. David lay panting and rolled onto his back in the graveyard. Dark clouds swept across the sky, occasionally revealing a glimpse of the moon. There was dog shit on one hand. He wiped it on the grass and walked in the darkness past gravestones of long-forgotten locals to the back of the church where the van was parked.

He drove off, taking the back road through Hartpury. A few miles further up the road, he pulled over into a layover bay. He pulled the mask off at last. The cold night breeze suddenly chilled his sweaty head. He removed boots, coat, shirt, trousers, and socks. He placed all clothes in a garbage bag and, with fresh gloves on, put on new clothes, then fitted the 'John' mask.

Sitting in the van, he pulled out the large scissors and, with gloved hands, the Ogden mask. *Here goes four grand,* he thought as he cut the mask into pieces roughly an inch across and put them in a plastic bag that had vinegar in it. When the mask was fully desiccated, he swirled and scrunched the pieces in the vinegar to wash them of any of his sweat. Then he carefully put a handful of pieces into each of about 20 small paper bags. Also, in separate paper bags went the used gloves and the bag that the knife was in. In the bottom of the sports bag, he found the button he had removed from the coat in Paris and a sewing kit. He replaced the button and made a neat repair of the tear in the tail flap.

Driving back roads to Cardiff, David stopped wherever there was a bin and put one of the paper bags of mask pieces in each bin, always hiding it from view where possible. *No one will take any notice of a paper bag in their bin.*

He arrived in Cardiff around midnight and went to the 24-hour laundrette he had scoped earlier that day. Saturday night. People were out and about, but it seemed none were doing their laundry. He washed all the clothes he had been wearing when he killed price on the heavy setting. His eyes hurt. The mask was way uncomfortable. Sitting on the hard bench in the laundrette, he fought off sleep as the time passed painfully slowly. It was after 2.30 am when the drier finally stopped. David carefully folded them and placed each garment in a separate fresh garbage bag.

David then drove to a Salvation Army donation bin and dumped the bagged clothes.

Driving into the Neath Port Talbot hospital car park about 4:15 am, sleep was pushing him down like a heavy weight on his head. David felt his heart racing as adrenalin stress set in. There was not a soul around as he took the bike from the back of the van. Legs aching as he pushed the pedals, the chill night air penetrated his jacket, like a cold knife against his chest, bringing the vision of Price's dead eyes to his memory. *Did I really do that? Maybe it was all a dream, and I'll wake up warm and comfortable in the cottage, and today will be like any other.* David faded back to reality *No. I have a latex mask on, and I'm riding through the night. I killed a man. A man that deserved to die. Justice has been served.*

He removed the 'John' mask on the narrow, sealed track to the farm and stashed it in his backpack. He continued to the farm and carried the bike over the sandy track, again walking on the grassy verge. Chill wind pushed in relentlessly from the sea, blowing the trees and the sand. *There won't be any sign of my tracks in a half an hour.* The light was growing in the east behind the hills. It was still quite dark, but David didn't turn any lights on until it was approaching 6 am. The urge to lie down and sleep was overpowering his will to stay awake, but he had to complete the illusion that he never left the cottage last night. He knew Mrs. J would be out for a walk around 7.00. He had to be seen by her this morning. Eyes closed involuntarily, he jolted himself awake, splashed cold water on his face. He checked his reflection. He looked like death warmed up. *Just another hour or so, then I'll be ok. Keep going, Dave.* He told himself. *Almost there.* At 6.30, David put on his morning walking gear and headed to the beach.

The wind had eased a little, but it was cold. Rolls of sea foam encrusted with sand and fragments of seaweed cartwheeled up the beach to the high tide line. He walked on the firm, wet sand to make it easier. Everything seemed to be moving, rotating in his view. Every patch of soft sand looked like a comfortable place to sleep and seemed to be calling him to stop and rest. *Keep walking. One step after another. I can do this.*

Mrs. J still hadn't appeared as David made his way up from the beach towards the cottage. He would have to wait for her—a while at least. He was longing for sleep - his whole body was beginning to feel very heavy, eyes burning. Finally, as he stood looking back at the sea, he heard Mrs. J's door close. He kept facing the ocean until she passed behind him and advised him to get the fire going.

In the cottage, sleep was screaming at him, but there were still a few things to attend to.

He had only just got the fire started when Mick Judd rang.

With Mick on the way to see him, sleep would have to wait another 20 minutes.

David removed all the timers from the lamps in the living room and bedroom and the stereo unit.

He carefully removed all the pins that set the start and stop times from the timers and reset them to random times. He put them all in a box with the other extension cords and spare light globes that Mrs. J kept on the top shelf in the storeroom.

He removed a cassette from the old stereo player in the living room and threw it into the fire. He watched as it contorted and twisted in the flames before erupting into a fireball, sending acrid black smoke up the chimney. Eventually, it was just a boiling, smoking black blob on the burning log, and then it was gone.

He took some dishes from the cupboard and set them in the drying rack on the sink. He put a couple of drops of whiskey from a half-empty bottle in a shot glass and set it with the bottle on the coffee table.

Standing at the bedroom door, he surveyed the scene in the room. Everything looked in order. He set his alarm and lay down to sleep. The vision of Price's dead body flashed in his mind as he dozed off. He had killed him—justice for Marion at last. A wave of contentment and righteousness flowed through his body and mind as he fell asleep.

****

Part 6. Revelation

The next day, Monday, David was returning from his beach walk when he met Mrs. J. on the path.

"Good Morning Mrs. J, a bit nicer weather today."

"Yes, certainly is. What's on your agenda today?"

"Well, I thought I might ride into town and catch the train down to Cardiff for the day. Probably won't get many days as nice as this while I'm here. Which brings me to another question – will it be ok for me to stay till Thursday? I haven't got much writing done yet. A couple of extra days would be great."

"No problem, David. Nobody else booked in until Monday. Say, what was the story with the detective yesterday? Why was he asking about you?"

"Bit of a strange one, that. Apparently, someone got murdered in my village at the same place Marion was killed. They wanted to know if I knew anything about it. It was exactly a year later—a strange coincidence. I expect all the local gossip troupe will have all the answers by the time I get back."

"I see. Have a good day, then. Bye."

"And you have a good day too, Mrs. J. I should be back in the afternoon sometime. Bye."

Mrs. J continued down the path to the beach. David returned to the cottage, packed a backpack with the John mask, a couple of ham and cheese sandwiches, and a small flask of tea. He left his phone on the charger on the bedside table. He took the best bicycle, wheeling it along the sandy track to the gate. He rode along the sealed road, stopping at a cluster of trees to don the mask unseen. He rode into Port Talbot and chained the bike up in the rack outside the Railway Station. He walked across to the hospital carpark to where the van was parked.

He drove the main highways to Cheltenham. Shortly before Gloucester, he turned off the A40 into 2 Mile Lane, and stopping near a farm gate, he removed the mask and stashed it back in his backpack.

At Peter's office, he returned the keys to Liz. "Peter in?"

"No, sorry, he's just gone to lunch not 10 minutes ago."

"Blast! Oh well, no issue, really. I'll call him and thank him. Bye Liz."

Between Peter's office and the railway station, the Landsdown Industrial Estate provided a hidden spot behind a vacant building for David to put John back on. He used cash to buy a fresh Oyster Card for the trip back to Port Talbot.

Green fields slowly passed in the distance as trees and poles flashed past the train windows. David closed his eyes and leaned back in his seat. Light and dark pulsed on his eyelids as objects passed the train windows, lulling him into deep relaxed thought. The shell of a mischievous plot was starting to gel. He would tell the story of how he pulled off the deception in the guise of a fictional narrative. Details and names would need to be changed, of course, to make sure he was never found out. Apart from it being a juicy story, there was another motive – to expose the paradox of proof and truth. The paradox that would have had Marion's murderer go unpunished. And the paradox that would see justice done in the end.

Cold sea air buffeted bike and rider on the way back to the cottage. The shelter of the cluster of trees was a welcome relief as well as a place to remove the mask. The wind on David's sweaty face was uncomfortably cold. *That's you done, John. Thanks, but I'll have to kill you tomorrow.* David thought as he studied the distorted, eyeless mask in his hand.

That night, he wrote into the small hours.

By the following Thursday, a sizable chunk of David Croswell's latest crime fiction was mapped out. Except that it wasn't entirely fiction. It was a commentary on how he had killed Price and set Ogden up to take the fall. The names were changed, of course, and details altered—no mention of a trip to Milan, no borrowing a van, a hire car was substituted. But it nonetheless told the complete story of how the deception was made and how the technology the police use to find criminals can be used to obscure the truth and create false evidence. David really liked the story.

He got home to Maisemore on Thursday afternoon and walked down to the White Horse for a meal and a refreshment.

"Nasty business last weekend." He said to Barry at the bar. "What is the goss around town?"

"The cops have been all over the place – but I don't know if they've found much. Your mate Ogden seems to be getting a lot of attention. They came and got a copy of my CCTV files, but there'd be nothing on them. I didn't see Price or Ogden here that night."

"Can I have a look at it?"

"Sure, but they are probably overwritten by now. It only stores about four days' worth. Come out to the office, and I'll show you."

At the computer, Barry opened the CCTV files. "I'd better get back to the bar, but have a look for yourself. Give me a shout if you need anything."

David scanned the files. Sure enough, the video from Saturday night had already been overwritten. Then he saw another file—the IR images. Looking through them, he found the images from Saturday night at the time he looked up at the camera. It was absolutely clear what it showed. Only the eyes and mouth showed up bright. The rest of his head was black. He was obviously wearing a mask.

****

In the reflection on his computer screen one afternoon, David saw Judy's silver BMW pulling into his driveway.

"Hello, darling. I didn't know you were coming over."

"No. Sorry, I just thought I'd drop in. Actually, Dad, there's something I need to talk to you about."

"Sure, Jude. Would you like some tea?"

"Yes, please."

"What did you want to talk about?" David asked as he returned from the kitchen with 2 cups and sat opposite Judy.

Judy thought for a moment. "I was talking to Shirley yesterday – you know, James's sister. And she asked me how you got on with moving stuff—when you borrowed one of Peter's old vans. You never mentioned to me that you were doing that."

"No, well, I thought I'd avoid any offers of help."

"But dad, that's not what bothers me. What bothers me is *when* she said you borrowed it. It was the same weekend you were away in Port Talbot...... and that's the same weekend that Daniel Price was killed. You see what I mean? Why would you have borrowed a van on that weekend.... You weren't even here. At first, I thought Shirl must have got the dates wrong, but she insisted that was right. It was two weeks before they sold them at the auction house. You see why I'm worried about this, dad. What did you do that weekend?"

133

David looked at his daughter's concerned face. It was useless to try to lie to her. He could lie to Mick Judd with carefully predetermined scenarios, but Judy knew him far too well.

"Don't worry, Jude. I've covered my tracks."

"DAD!!! WHAT DID YOU DO? DID YOU KILL PRICE? FUCKING HELL, DAD! YOU COULD GET A LENGTHY JAIL TERM. WHAT WERE YOU THINKING? WHAT IF YOU GET FOUND OUT?"

Judy was pacing the room. "Fuck, Dad. Why did you do that? Jesus!"

David was all in now. "YES, I KILLED THAT PRICK. I PLANNED IT, I FOLLOWED THROUGH, AND HE FUCKING PAID WITH HIS LIFE! ...... He called mum a 'stupid cow' in one of his texts. Fucking 'Stupid Cow'??, I thought. I'll fucking show you who's fucking stupid!"

"DAD!! YOU ARE A MURDERER! HOW COULD YOU DO THAT??"

"It wasn't easy. I couldn't believe it myself afterwards. But I had to find my peace. I couldn't live the rest of my life with the agony of knowing your mother's killer was walking around free, thinking he had got away with it."

Judy sat down again. "But how can you be sure he did it?"

"He surely did. And I got him to record his confession on his own phone before I…... before he left this world."

Judy sat in silence, digesting the situation. "And Ogden. Did you fit him up for it?"

"Err… yes. He was in mum's murder up to his eyeballs. He had his chance, to tell the truth, but instead, he chose to back Price up. So, he had to pay, too."

"I can't believe that you …….my father …… is a murderer. I can't deal with this. I love you, dad, but fucking hell …..killing someone …….I don't know what to think. I'm going home."

Judy snatched up her coat, and stormed out, and drive off with spinning wheels on the gravel. She was clearly not pleased to discover that her father was a murderer.

David lay in bed that night staring at the ceiling. *Would Judy talk to me again? Have I blown the whole thing now? What if she says something to James? This could get really ugly. What if she goes to Judd?*

The thought of going to jail and not seeing his grandchildren grow up was cutting him deep. *Judy has to understand that I just had to do this, or live in torment my whole life.* He thought of calling her but thought better of it. *I've done the deed. What I had to do. I knew there was a risk. I chose the path anyway.*

****

When Judy arrived home, she stormed through the house and went straight to the bedroom.

"What's the matter, darling?" James called after her.

"I need some time to think. I can't tell you …. yet."

"Ok ………. If you need to talk about it, I'm here."

An hour later, Judy emerged from the bedroom and sat in silence on the couch, staring at the cover of a book on the coffee table.

James watched her from the kitchen. "Tea?"

No response came from Judy.

"I'll make it anyway." James continued, putting the kettle on.

He shortly arrived with two cups of tea and placed them on the table; and sat opposite his wife, who had tears on her cheeks. He could feel that she needed some space.

After a few minutes silence, she began. "It's dad. He's done something stupid."

"He wouldn't be the only one. And probably not the first time for him either."

"No. This is something really, really stupid."

"Oh. Do you want to tell me?"

"No, I don't. But I think I am going to have to tell you anyway. It's not a secret I would want to keep from you."

"Well??"

Judy took a deep breath and sighed. "Well, you know how William Ogden got convicted for murdering Daniel Price?"

"Yes, of course. They had heaps of concrete evidence that he did it."

"I know. But he *didn't* kill Price. ....Dad *did*!" Judy burst into tears. James moved over to her and put his arms around her, holding her tight as she sobbed uncontrollably. "He killed Price and set Ogden up to go down for it!"

"Jesus! That *is* serious." James waited for Judy to stop crying, arms around her shoulders, rocking her gently and kissing her temple. After a few minutes, Judy had almost stopped crying.

"What do you want to do?" James asked.

"I don't know." Judy relied, almost in a whisper. "He did it for what were the right reasons for him – not really revenge, more getting justice he couldn't get from the courts."

"Darling, you know the game. You have defended people that you know have committed a crime. That's the way the system works. You know that. You are part of it. I think we can all kid ourselves that we are doing the right thing, when it's our job. You do it. I do it." James paused to collect his thoughts. "In the hospital, you know, when a patient is dying from a terminal disease. We help them along. It's called Pain Relief. A bit of extra morphine and they are done with this life. To be absolutely blunt, we kill them. Euthanasia, by another name. It's what the patient wants. It's what the family wants. It's not strictly legal, but we justify it on the basis that we are relieving the pain of living with something unbearable. Is it right or wrong? It's a fine line. At the end of the day, we need to be able to live our lives feeling that we have done the right thing. ………….. I think your dad was living with the pain of something unbearable. Not a terminal illness, although that's what it could have become if it went on long enough. He had to do it, or he was dead inside and your mom's killer was alive. He was handed a life sentence of resentment the day Price was acquitted. The justice system couldn't deliver him relief, so he had to find it himself."

Judy was beginning to see things in a different light. She had been there herself. After Price was acquitted, she actually had thoughts of killing Price herself. But that's as far as it went. "We absolutely know that Price killed mum. Dad got him to do a video where he admitted to killing mum. On Price's own phone."

James held Judy gently but firmly. "What shall we do, Jude. It's your call."

"What do *you* think?"

"I think we should talk to you dad about this. Personally, I am kinda full of admiration for him. That's a *way* gutsy thing to do. I want to know how he did it so he wouldn't get caught.

"Alright. I'll call him tomorrow. We'll go and see him."

The next morning, Judy called David. He hadn't slept much, and nor had she. "Dad, James and I are coming over tonight. Cook us up something for dinner. We need to have a serious talk with you."

"Alright, Darling. Six o'clock?"

"More like six thirty. We are getting a sitter."

"See you then, bye."

She sounded happier. David thought. *Clearly, she has told James. I don't think she is going to the police. Maybe she will want me to turn myself in? I don't think I could do that. I'll wait and see what they have to say to me.*

At 6.36 that evening, Judy and James arrived at the door. David was apprehensive, trying to read the mood. Judy and James were both much less jovial that usual.

"Sit down" David said, indicating the dining table. "I've made a vegan mushroom risotto. What would you like to drink.?"

"Red please." James and Judy said in unison.

They ate in near silence, small talk conspicuously absent. There was a heavy tension in the room.

Eventually, Judy spoke. "Dad. I have told James what you told me. We have had talk about it. I want you to know first up that your secret is safe with us, it's not going any further."

David looked visibly relieved.

"We understand. Getting justice for mum – the only way you could. The only way at all. But we are worried. Worried that you will get found out. We need to know what you did – all of it. We need to know if there is anything you have missed that would land you in the frame. So, tonight you are going to tell us everything. No matter how long it takes. All the details, what you did, where you went, everything, ok. We might need to open another bottle of red – or two. Let's get these dishes in the dishwasher and get started."

For the next 3 hours, Judy and James sat in awe as David described the whole process—the masks, the pickpocket, the texts, everything. He went into all the details of how he made sure that he never left and fingerprints or DNA on anything he touched. How he had gone to Milan, leaving his phone in Paris to make it appear as though he stayed there. He described how he had changed masks to obscure his identity at every point. He detailed how he had made sure that Mrs. J was absolutely convinced that he was there the whole Saturday night, so that she would be doubly convincing to Judd when he questioned her. How he wore Ogden's boots and the sealed socks how he carried Ogden's phone to the murder scene, and how he had glanced at the White Horse security camera to record that Ogden had been there. David explained how he had copied exactly Ogden's clothes, right down to the button detail and then washed and dried them before dropping them in the donation bin. He told of how he cut up and disposed of the Ogden mask even before he got back to Port Talbot, and had posted the John mask to a non-existent address in Bolivia with no return address. David described how he used his knowledge of police investigation techniques to make it appear that he was where he wasn't and wasn't where he was. How he made false number plates for the van that matched a similar van he had seen in Gloucester.

"The only thing that bothers me now is that Shirley might know that the weekend I borrowed the van was the same weekend Price was killed. You didn't tell her I was at Port Talbot that weekend, did you?"

"No, I didn't mention it." Judy said. "It only dawned on me after… on my way home. That's when I got worried."

"I just hope that CID doesn't get wind of it. It's probably the weakest link in my plan. Judd has been asking questions – they had heaps of evidence against Ogden – I made sure of that. But he's a hardened D. He has an inkling that something's not right – and that I had something to do with it. But even if they did find out about the van, there's still no way they can prove I'm guilty - It's all covered."

"Remember, I'm a lawyer, dad. I'm good at finding the weaknesses in someone's story. Fuck, I hope you have this covered."

Judy had some questions. "What about CCTV at the Hospital Carpark?"

"None. I checked it out thoroughly."

"What about Traffic Monitors on the highways?

"I dodged them—used back roads and bypasses. Anyway, put false plates on the van. Copied a number from a similar one in town."

After many more questions, Judy was convinced. She looked long and hard at her father. He had done the only thing that could set him free from a life of torment and regret. He had not just thought about it. He had done it! *My father is a murderer, he killed Price for his peace, and justice for mum. And for me. He's a killer, but a loving, caring, gentle father. I just love him so much, I could cry.*

"You are a legend, dad. I love you so much. Mum would be proud of you. You know, I actually feel like a weight has been lifted from me, knowing we finally got justice for mum. Just a pity you had to go outside the law to get it."

Well, Jude – you are the lawyer. You know how the law works – and how it doesn't work. That's what my new book is about."

"What do you mean?"

"I'm writing my story – *our* story of this whole nightmare and redemption – to show just how the law can fail."

"You're telling the story of how you killed Price!? Isn't that a bit risky?"

"It's a fictional narrative. Fits with my last two books. All the details are changed, so it can't be traced back to the real events. I think I've got it covered. Judd may get the connection, but he won't be able to prove anything."

"You're a wily old fox, dad."

"Thanks"

"Well, in the light of all that, I think this calls for a celebration. What have you got?" James announced.

"I have a bottle of Dom Perignon that I was going to have with mum on our anniversary – the one she never made it to. I suppose that would be apropos."

"Perfect!"

David fetched the bottle from the cellar fridge and three champagne flutes.

"Let's drink to mum. And to justice." Judy said, raising her glass.

"Poetic Justice. To Marion. May her beauty and compassion always be an inspiration to us."

"Cheers!"

Part 7. Resolution

In November that year, Michael Judd arrived at work to find a small package on his desk. The attached card simply read, *'Enjoy! Regards, Dave.'*

It was a book—David Croswell's latest release, personally signed, entitled 'The Proof Trap'.

Judd started to read the book the following weekend, and although he didn't read a lot of books and never read crime fiction, this one, he couldn't put down. Much to his wife Karen's displeasure, he abandoned all planned chores and read. Read until it was finished, in the small hours of Sunday morning. When he put the book down at 3.22 am, he was highly disturbed by what he had read. It turned his world on its head, caused him to question everything he had done in his career, left him feeling perplexed and frustrated. The final words in the book would stay with him for the rest of his life.

'That which is true, but cannot be proven so, becomes not true.

And that which is not true, yet is proven to be true, becomes the truth.

****

It was a rainy Friday afternoon when David heard the doorbell. At the door was Mick Judd, holding the copy of "The Proof Trap".

"Come in, Mick. Great to see you. Coffee? Or something stronger?

"What have you got anything in single malt?

"18-year-old Glenfiddich. Will that do?"

"Perfect."

"Have a seat, Mick. Did you like it?" David asked, referring to the book.

Mick Judd sat in the corner of the 'L' shaped sofa as David poured two large glasses of whiskey. "Ice?"

"No, thanks."

David handed Mick his whiskey and sat in the recliner opposite. The book was on the table between them.

Mick sipped his whiskey and turned his eyes to the book. "No. I fucking hated it."

"Really? Why?"

"Because it is what I face all the time ......finding proof. Finding proof of things and not knowing if it's true. Satisfying the court process. Now you have described just how wrong it can be ..... just how much we can get it wrong. Especially if someone deliberately sets out to fool us."

"Well, it was kind of the purpose of the book. We all knew Price killed Marion. And it was true but not proven. The problem is that, with the presumption of innocence, when the proof of guilt cannot be found, they are pronounced to be innocent. But Price wasn't innocent. He was still guilty, even if the proof of that guilt couldn't be found. The book was just exploring and exposing this paradox."

"And what about Ogden? He was proven guilty even though he was innocent – of the crime he was charged with at least."

"Exactly. That's the second paradox. But are you absolutely sure he was innocent – that he didn't kill Price?"

"Almost."

"But not definitely?"

"No. not definitely."

Judd sipped his whiskey and stared into the middle distance for a minute.

You did it, didn't you?" Judd said at last.

"Did what?"

"Murdered Price and set Ogden up to take the fall – just like in your book."

"It's fiction, Mick. Loosely based on a true story with a lot of imagination thrown in."

"You know, Dave. I don't believe you. I think you did it."

"Well, we both know that sometimes what we think we know to be true cannot be proved. Do you think you can prove I did it?"

"Not a snowball's chance in hell. I've spent the past three months trying to find even the slightest hint of anything that I could use as evidence – even knowing the exact method used. I checked with every mask maker in Amsterdam and Paris, and none had ever seen or heard of you. I've checked all the car hire businesses in the southwest. I've tested every possible weak link."

"What drove you to look for evidence, Mick? Was it a sense of duty to restore justice, or just curiosity?

"A bit of both, I suppose. And the force of habit. But mostly, I just wanted to be comfortable that I knew the truth, irrespective of the law and what could be proven."

"And how did you go with that?"

"Terribly. I still have nothing tangible to back up my belief."

"Don't let that spoil your day, Mick. Billions of religious followers around the world are in the same boat." David quipped. "Anyway, Ogden was proven guilty beyond all reasonable doubt. You provided the proof to the court. Didn't you believe he was guilty?"

"I had a lingering doubt for a long time. But I think I convinced myself in the end to close the case. I was happy with the result.... until I read your book. As I see it, there is a man in prison who did not commit the crime, and I have not one shred of evidence to support that contention, and a killer running free with not a shred of evidence to convict them."

"Well, as far as I can see, Mick, you are faced with a paralysing professional quandary. If what is not true can be absolutely proven to be true, and what was is true can be proven to be untrue, where does that leave you in the search for the truth?"

Judd took a large swig of whiskey, swirled it in his mouth, and swallowed.

"Fucked." He stared at his glass, swirling the remaining amber fluid. "I have nightmares where I question every judgment, every conviction I've ever got across the line. Thanks a lot, pal."

"You are most welcome. But what about the question of moral victory here? Hypothetically, if a man kills an innocent woman out for an evening stroll, he goes to court and gets acquitted, and his accomplice in the murder gets off scot-free. The woman's husband conspires to murder the man and have the accomplice take the fall. What's your take on the morality of that hypothetical scenario?"

"It would seem right. But my life has been dedicated to upholding the *law*, not morality."

"What's more important – law or morality?"

Judd thought for a moment, staring at his glass.

"Morality. The law is designed to support a high moral order."

"But does it always succeed? That's the quandary."

"No. Not always."

"So, in those cases where the law fails, how can the moral order be restored?"

"Well, I suppose, if the law fails, then the moral balance can only be restored outside the law."

"I think you've nailed it, Mick. The law failed Marion. And me. And Judy and my grandchildren. Any other questions the book raised for you?"

"Just one. The story has all the elements of the real case, except one piece of the puzzle that wasn't in there. The text message to Judy from Swansea. How could that be possible if you were in Maisemore murdering Price?"

"Remember, the book is fiction, Mick. It's the character, Brian, in the book, not me. Brian could only have sent that message by being in Swansea. That's why I left it out of the book. I just couldn't work out how Brian could have done that."

"So, you are in the clear, innocent? Nothing in your book really happened?"

"Here's something for you to ponder, Mick. What if there is something important that you have missed? Something that proved Ogden was actually innocent. Hypothetically, what if there was some truth in my story?"

"I guess you'd be testing my detective skills."

"Yes. But what else? If you *did* find that evidence? Where would your loyalties fall?"

"I'd have a difficult choice to make. Morality, friendship, law. It's murky."

"Quite."

"Are you saying there is some evidence out there that I haven't found?"

"Just a hypothetical, Mick. Make your own call on it."

"It is just such a massive task. To what end? Cash transactions, deliberately staged phone locations, long overwritten CCTV files, I have no resources to pursue any leads anyway, even if I did find a thread. How far and wide would I have to look to find this missing link?"

"You need to be careful about looking too far out. Sometimes we can't see what is under our noses."

"You're fucking with my head, Dave."

"Another whiskey, Mick?" David grinned.

****

It was well passed office hours, and the CID office was dark. All but one had gone home. Michael Judd leaned back in his office chair, a whiskey bottle on the desk amongst several files and a half-empty glass in his hand. The wall clock behind him ticked noisily in the silent office. What was it David had said to him the previous Saturday? *Sometimes we can't see what is under our noses.*

He put down the glass and opened the 'Closed Cases' folder in the CID archives, and opened the 'Daniel Price' evidence file on his computer. He flicked though the various file names looking for something that might contain something he missed. *'Sometimes we can't see what is under our noses'.* David had said. The folder 'White Horse CCTV' caught his attention. *'what is under our noses'.* He opened the folder. It contained two files. One was the video file they had used to identify Ogden in the carpark. The other, they had never looked at – considering it irrelevant. It was the IR imagery, InfraRed recording made by the night vision camera.

As he played it through, it showed the Infra-red or heat emission pattern from the people in the picture – mostly from exposed areas such as head and hands. To his amazement, when Ogden looked up at the camera, the only heat spots were his mouth and eyes. The rest of his head and shoulders were black. That person was wearing a head and shoulders mask—just like in Dave's book! It wasn't Ogden at all! And the eyewitness had not seen him either, but a masked imposter!

Judd leaned back, looking at the ceiling. After several minutes, he picked up his phone. It was 7.46 pm. He called David.

"Hello, Dave. I found it. That wasn't Ogden crossing the carpark."

"Well done. What does it prove?"

"It proves, it wasn't him who had his phone, so it wasn't him that killed Price. You could have been the man under the mask. Or it might have been someone else. You knew what was happening, at least."

"Did I really, Mick? I could just have made a lucky guess in my book, but actually, I saw the IR file too. You see, after I learned of Price's murder, my crime writer mind started looking for clues. When I got back from Port Talbot, I went to see Barry to ask who was around that night and asked to see what was on his CCTV. Unfortunately, the video file memory only stores about four days of video, so the Saturday night file was already overwritten. But because the IR image files are much smaller, there's about two weeks' worth of images stored. So, I took a copy home with me to see if there was anything on it that might give any clues, but it's hard to identify anyone from an IR file. I didn't really know what I was looking at – at the time. I looked at it again after Ogden's trial. That's when I realised that the person crossing the carpark that night was wearing a mask. That's where I got the idea for my story."

"So, why didn't you tell me about this evidence?"

"It was a while after Ogden's conviction before I understood it myself. Anyway, what would be in it for me? It's not proof of who

153

the murderer is. We don't know who was under the mask. But we know that whoever it was, they were likely to be the murderer. And why would I want to protect Ogden, after he lied to get Price off for Marion's murder? I was pretty happy for him to take the fall."

"You're right. What-ifs and maybes. Not *proof*. But now I think I know the truth, Dave."

"You're the detective, Mick. You will have your beliefs about what is true and what is not. And what you can prove and what you can't. The real question is - what will you do with it?"

"I don't know, Dave. I'll have to think about it. Bye."

"Bye, Mick, I'm sure whatever you do will be the right thing."

Judd played the IR file again. *Absolutely no doubt about it. The person in the carpark that night was wearing a mask. Ogden was innocent – of Price's murder at least. But still he had a hand in Marion's murder, lied to police, and in court. He had gone unpunished for that. But more importantly, he could have told the truth and got Price convicted for killing Marion. Then none of this would have happened. In a way, he contributed to Price's murder, even though he wasn't there.*

His detective mind kicked in automatically. *What could this thread lead to? What else was out there? What would it prove? Where is the mask now? It must be somewhere. It would have the possible killer's DNA on it. That could lead us to a whole new line of enquiry or follow up the existing one - if it was Croswell in the mask. Should I get a warrant to search David's place for the mask? If he disposed of it as described in the book, we have not the slightest chance of finding it. It all would have been incinerated months ago.*

Then the human took over. *Hasn't justice, however crude, been served here anyway? Closer to a moral resolution than our legal system managed. What misery would he need to put himself and Dave through to pursue it - for the uncertain result? Could he do this to Dave, anyway? Hasn't Dave suffered enough? Ogden could have avoided his situation by not lying about Marion. He made his choice and now he's paying for it.*

And eventually, Judd, the career policeman, got a say. *If this piece of evidence is reviewed by someone else, will that start an investigation? Would I then be in the frame for overlooking it? That possibility could only be eliminated by deleting the file. But if I did, it could be found that I deleted it and when. What was the lesser of the evils? But seriously, there's near zero chance anyone will ever look here again.*

Judd finished the glass of whiskey and was about to pour another when he stopped. He pushed the cork back in the bottle and returned it to his bottom desk drawer. He highlighted the file name for the IR file and pressed DELETE.

A message came up on the screen:

155

"Are you sure you want to permanently delete this file?

This action cannot be undone."

He hovered the mouse over the CANCEL button for at least a minute. Suddenly, he moved it across to YES and clicked it.

It was done.

He closed the computer, turned off the lights, and went home. Driving home he thought about his decision. *So, Ogden did not kill Price, so who did? Could it have been Dave? Maybe. He had the strongest motive of anyone. Or Judy? Didn't seem at all likely. There's no way she could have hog tied him. Or someone else altogether? Where could I start with that? No-one else at all came up in the investigation.* Despite all that his instincts were telling him, there was still one hitch - David could not possibly have killed Price because he was in the Port Talbot cottage at the time. He had to be there to turn the record over and send the text to Judy.

He pulled into his driveway and turned off the car and lights. Sitting for a few minutes, leaned his head back on the headrest. *I need a break. Karen is right .... I've got months of long service leaving owing. You know what? Fuck this job. I'm going to take Karen and go to Australia. See what Jordie is doing. Come back refreshed.......... maybe.*

****

At 9.53 pm on the 13th May earlier that year, in a beachside cottage out of Port Talbot, a mechanical timer in the power socket switched to 'ON', feeding power to the stereo unit and the cassette player, which had the play button activated. The Pink Floyd album "Dark Side of The Moon' played through. Then, after some silence, at 10.43, the voice of David Croswell came from the speakers. *"Hey Siri, send a message to Judy"*. After a pause for the phone on the sideboard to respond, the voice continued. *"Hi Jude, I hope you are coping ok tonight. In hindsight, I maybe should have stayed home rather than come down here. I've not had much luck writing with Mum on my mind. Anyway, I'm off to bed now, the waves are crashing against the shore, that will help me sleep. I'll call you tomorrow, ok. Goodnight darling – love you very much."*

****